# LETTERS OF CICERO

Classical History and Literature

Editor
PROFESSOR H. T. WADE-GERY
F B A
formerly *Wykeham Professor of Ancient History*
*in the University of Oxford*

# LETTERS OF CICERO

## A SELECTION IN TRANSLATION

## L. P. Wilkinson

Fellow of King's College, Cambridge

HUTCHINSON UNIVERSITY LIBRARY
LONDON

HUTCHINSON & CO *(Publishers)* LTD
*178–202 Great Portland Street, London W1*

London Melbourne Sydney
Auckland Bombay Toronto
Johannesburg New York

*First published by
Geoffrey Bles Ltd 1949
Arrow edition 1959
This edition 1966*

*This book has been set in Fournier, printed in Great Britain
on Smooth Wove paper by Anchor Press, and
bound by Wm. Brendon, both of Tiptree, Essex*

to
MY WIFE

# CONTENTS

# MAPS

## PREFACE TO 1966 EDITION

In this edition for the Hutchinson University Library I have made
some alterations suggested by Dr D. R. Shackleton Bailey's edition
of *Ad Atticum I-IV* with commentary (Cambridge University Press,
1965).

L.P.W.

*July 1965*

## PREFACE TO 1959 EDITION

In this new edition I have made a number of alterations. I have
consulted the text and translation of the incomplete Budé edition of
Constans and Bayet, and the new text of the Italians Moicca and Caputo.
On a very few points I have troubled Dr D. R. Shackleton Bailey, for
whose help I am grateful: if I had had the face to ask more, I should
not have known where to stop. At proof stage I have also been able
to consult the new *Oxford Classical Text* of the letters to Quintus and
Brutus by Professor W. S. Watt.

L.P.W.

*August 1958*

# PREFACE TO 1949 EDITION

For various reasons the letters of Cicero are less well known to the reading public than they deserve to be. Many of them require more background and explanation than the layman would think it worth while to acquire, and many are of secondary interest. For the general reader selection is therefore inevitable, though it involves the loss of one of the chief merits of the corpus as a whole, the cumulative effect, the sense of sharing a man's life and thoughts from day to day; and since these are genuine letters, not essays in epistolary form, I have often left out parts of letters that are less interesting or intelligible. The present selection is intended primarily for readers who are not conversant with the classics. Its aim is to avoid what would require too much explanation and yet to give a representative impression of Cicero's career and character, of life in his day, and of the changing political scene.

After a general introduction the events of Cicero's life previous to the first letter chosen are summarised in a few pages. Thereafter, with the aid of short narrative links and occasional footnotes, the reader will, I hope, be able to follow the course of events and the drift of each letter. There are, however, so many points that might seem to require explanation, that he must be asked to take it on trust that anything left unexplained is immaterial to the present purpose. Where the text is doubtful, I have made my choice of reading and said nothing. There is a map of Italy on p. 29, a map of the Eastern Mediterranean on p. 158, and a glossary of technical terms and an index of proper names at the end of the book.

No translation can hope to do justice to the terse economy of

Cicero's Latin; but I have tried to get away from 'translation' English and to give the reader the same impression as I think a contemporary Roman would have received. Occasionally, I have been a little more explicit than the original, for the sake of avoiding a footnote. Where I have been free, I hope I have not been unfaithful.

There are several special problems to be faced. For instance, Greek was a second language to educated Romans as no language is to us, and Cicero, especially when writing to Atticus, drops easily into Greek words and phrases. Roman culture had been imported from Greece in the previous century, and Latin had not evolved many technical terms or refinements of vocabulary. Sometimes an acclimatised French, or even Latin, word may give the right impression to an Englishman; but more often it would sound too affected to use anything but English jargon. Similarly with the numerous quotations: sometimes a genuine English quotation may produce the right effect, but more often a plausible invention will serve. Dates have been converted to our system throughout, save for the famous *Ides of March*. Names of people are anglicised if they are household words—Pompey, Mark Antony. Names of places are generally modernised if they have a modern equivalent—Naples, Anzio; although this may sometimes sound a little discordant, the balance is in favour of enabling readers to recognise at once places they may happen to know. On the other hand I have called the former second city of Italy Capua, and not Santa Maria del Grazie. The one principle that would be wrong is consistency.

In my narrative links I have refrained from comment. It is better to say nothing than too little, and it would swell the book to unmanageable proportions if on every issue the case for both sides were put in full, while the letters themselves, which I want to throw into relief, would be buried under the debris.

The following books are recommended to those who wish to read more about Cicero and his times in the light of these letters:

J. L. Strachan-Davidson: *Life of Cicero* (2nd edn. 1925)
G. Boissier: *Ciceron et Ses Amis* (1865) (Eng. Tr.: *Cicero and His Friends*)
G. C. Richards: *Cicero, a Study* (1935)
H. J. Haskell: *This was Cicero* (1942)

W. Warde Fowler: *Social Life at Rome in the Age of Cicero* (1908).

F. R. Cowell: *Cicero and the Roman Republic* (1948).

T. A. Dorey and others: *Cicero* (1965).

I have used the monumental Dublin edition of Tyrrell and Purser. For historical points I have generally relied on *The Cambridge Ancient History*. I have also consulted the translations of E. S. Shuckburgh, W. Glynn Williams (*Ad Familiares*, Loeb edn.), E. O. Winstedt (*Ad Atticum*, Loeb edn.) and G. E. Jeans (of Watson's selection), and the notes of Watson's, How's and A. L. Irvine's selections. To the last named, my old teacher and a connoisseur of the Letters, I am much indebted for his careful and expert reading of the proofs; and to another old friend of Charterhouse days, Miss M. B. Jameson, for the valuable criticisms she made in the capacity of representative layman. Finally, I should like to thank Mr Geoffrey Bles, who has shown himself not only a most considerate and encouraging publisher, but a Quintilius able to offer valuable criticisms from an intimate knowledge of the Letters.

L.P.W.

*August 1948*

# Introduction

We may search history until quite modern times without finding either a personality so intimately known to us as Cicero or a period so vividly real as the years that led up to the murder of Julius Caesar in 44 B.C. Both of these facts are due to the survival of nearly eight hundred of Cicero's letters, together with more than a hundred written to him by others. By a most fortunate chance a man of rare liveliness and literary gifts, whose very weaknesses—egotism, vanity, indiscretion, nervousness—broke down the barriers of reticence, was there to play the part of Chorus, and sometimes of Protagonist, in that fascinating and moving tragedy. The dramatic quality of those years, so striking to us who can see them in historical perspective, was realised even by the participants, one of whom, Caelius, wrote to Cicero just before the outbreak of the Civil War: 'Destiny is preparing a spectacle which you would find grand and diverting, if only you could watch it from above the danger.'

There was no regular postal system in those days. Either you sent a special messenger, or you waited until you could avail yourself of the messenger of some friend or public official. Consequently letters tended to be either hasty notes scribbled as the bearer waited on the doorstep, or long and studied compositions. Cicero loved writing letters: he always had steam to let off. He would take up his pen anywhere—at the road-side, at the dinner-table, in the Senate. He would write to Atticus, his intimate friend, financial adviser and political confidant, even when he had nothing to say, 'so as not to miss a day', and we find him even writing three times in one day. Sometimes he would dictate, preferably to Tiro, his devoted secretary, steward and future biographer, who was an expert at shorthand and could take down whole sentences at once. How much of the spontaneity of the letters we must owe to Tiro's quickness! The other amanuenses were slower. Poor Spintharus had to be fed syllable by syllable. But slowness too had its uses, and he was employed when an awkward letter had to be sent to the formidable scholar Varro, in which every word had to be weighed.

Cicero kept copies of the more important letters. He could reassure a friend who regretted having torn one up by mistake; and he could send a duplicate to Caesar of one that got wet on the journey to Gaul and arrived illegible. If he did not want the bearer to be able to read anything, he wrote in Greek; if more important people were to be kept in the dark, he used covert phrases, and even resorted to pseudonyms.

How and when the correspondence came to be published is a matter of conjecture.[1] Fifteen months before his death Cicero mentions that there is no collection of his letters, but that Tiro has about seventy, while a few more can be retrieved from Atticus; he wishes to 'vet' them before they are published. Now it is clear from the fewness that this was to be a selection. Probably it was to contain letters which, authenticated by their having actually been sent, duly dated, to prominent people, would show what motives had prompted his actions at every stage. No doubt he sometimes had it in mind when he wrote such letters that they might come in useful: it was a convenient method of putting things on record, or circulating a manifesto. An outstanding example is a letter many pages long which he wrote to Lentulus Spinther in 54 B.C. to justify his seemingly tortuous political course during the previous three years. There was nothing disingenuous in the project of publishing such a selection, unless we suppose that Cicero, in spite of the risk of being confronted with the originals, which might still be in the possession of his correspondents, was going to cook the letters in the light of after events. Caesar had been equally anxious to justify his conduct, only he chose a different literary device, writing the record of his campaigns in Gaul with an objectiveness of

1. It is generally surmised that the letters to Atticus were published in the reign of Nero. For the theories of M. Carcopino see the note at the end of this Introduction.

manner as of a plain soldier doing great things for Rome but innocent of political ambition.

For whatever reason, the proposed selection seems never to have come to anything. What we have is quite a different matter. It is abundantly clear that Cicero wrote most of the letters with no thought of publication at all, and fortunately for us he did not live to edit them. Whether creditable or discreditable to himself, his thoughts, fears and hopes come teeming out, shaped as they go by his ready wit and easy mastery of language. Whenever, and in whatever circumstances, the correspondence of Cicero was published, its survival after his death was beyond doubt due to the business-like care of Atticus and the devotion of Tiro. Copies of letters to a host of correspondents, to Atticus, to Quintus Cicero and to Brutus in particular, must have been procured. It is not impossible that Tiro, who lived to the age of a hundred, was able to see to the publication of the collections that have come down to us.

If we may attribute to these two the collection and arrangement, and perhaps also the publication, of the letters, it is notable that they had the intelligence and faith to believe that the reputation of one to whom they had been devoted would best be served if all the cards were put on the table. Had they decided otherwise, had they made a plausible selection, it would have been open to any hostile person to produce originals of letters they had suppressed, with far more damaging effect. And in any case, *tout comprendre, c'est tout pardonner.*

No less remarkable is the minute interest in human personality which the publication of this vast mass of miscellaneous detail pre-supposes. There is no cause, however, to be sceptical about it. One of the great Roman qualities was *humanitas*, a word which implies both interest in human beings and sympathetic understanding born of that interest. Why did Horace like reading the old Roman poet Lucilius? Because 'he long ago entrusted his secrets to his books as to faithful friends, turning elsewhere neither when things went well for him nor when they went badly; with the result that the man's whole life lies open as if it were painted in a picture'. There is probably no human document comparable with Cicero's letters until we come to those works, among which Rousseau's *Confessions* should perhaps be counted the first, that have caused and catered for the modern preoc-cupation with motives and states of mind. Here we have a man thinking

aloud, sometimes almost by 'free association'. 'I talk to you', he says
to Atticus, 'as though I were talking to myself.' No detail, no passing
thought, is too trivial to mention, and the censor within keeps nodding.
What a case-book for the psychologist!

But although the interest to which these letters appeal has been
strongest in the past century and a half, their greatest influence was
exercised six hundred years ago. That spring morning in 1345 when
Petrarch rediscovered the letters to Atticus, to Quintus and to Brutus,
probably in the Cathedral Library at Verona, was one of the most
momentous occasions of the Renaissance. In the Middle Ages Cicero,
like other worthies of antiquity, had come to be little more than *magni
nominis umbra*, the shadow of a great name. His books were often
mentioned, but his personality was little known. There were parts of
Tuscany where he had become legendary as a warrior chief who had
besieged in Fiesole and forced to surrender a rebel called 'Catellina'
(popular sympathy inclining, as usual, to the outlaw). But now his
true self suddenly came to life again through the letters, to fire the
imagination of the Humanists, who were just then beginning with
intense excitement to rediscover the fascination of man's individuality.
Under his influence their own letters to each other gradually ceased to
be stilted compositions and became human and spontaneous. Zielinski
has done well to remind us that 'the Renaissance was before all things
a revival of Cicero, and only after him and through him of the rest of
Classical antiquity'. Petrarch's first reaction was to write him an open
letter: 'Your letters, which I have searched for long and often, and
have now found where least I expected, I have read through with the
keenest interest. I have heard your voice, Cicero, in your copious talk,
in your frequent lamentations, in your continual changes; and though
I had long known you as an instructor of others, I have now at last
discovered what you were in yourself.'

Now many people today are in the state of Petrarch before he
found the letters. To them Cicero is no name to conjure with: it will
not start a spirit as soon as Caesar. Mention it to a sixth-form boy or
an undergraduate and what image will you evoke? Probably that of a
toga-clad figure attitudinising on a pedestal, or of a dusty-haired,
blank-eyed bust on a shelf in a museum. Or it may be an auricular
image, of rolling periods of rhetorical prose, superlatives of praise and
blame, indignant protestations, and apostrophes to the immortal Gods.

We have come face to face already with one of the chief barriers. Rhetoric is out of fashion. Only a theme as instant as war with an orator as vivid as Churchill can make people willingly listen to it. It is associated for the most part with unreality, insincerity, fustian. And yet it is commonly the speeches of Cicero that are first put before schoolboys, who cannot be expected to see them in the historical setting which alone can bring them to life. No wonder if they are repelled, perhaps never to return. The more fortunate may begin with one of the easier philosophic treatises, *On Old Age* or *On Friendship*. But even these may strike them only as sermons more competent and colourful than those to which they are accustomed to lend their ears. The misfortune is that they cannot begin with the letters, because the style and vocabulary are too singular to be easy enough for anyone who has not gone some way with Latin. A great misfortune it is, for if only their interest could be early caught by the letters, they might be tempted later to venture on the speeches and philosophic works at an age when they could appreciate them against their historical or philosophic background. I wish this book could do for them something of what that old manuscript at Verona did for Petrarch.

Shakespeare's *Julius Caesar* and *Antony and Cleopatra* have made English readers familiar with the climax of the story and its sequel; but his characters are lifted above real life by the atmosphere of poetic tragedy, so that they are still apt to remain a little unreal to those unaccustomed to making the necessary mental equations for themselves; and what schoolboy ever believed in the real existence of that Balbus (all too human in Cicero's letters) who built a wall to illustrate the use of subject, verb and object on page 1 of the old grammar? It was left for Bernard Shaw, in his *Caesar and Cleopatra*, to stress the essential humanity that went with 'the high Roman fashion'. Shaw's play would not seem so novel, almost blasphemous, to anyone who knew the period not through the tradition of Plutarch's *Lives of the Noble Grecians and Romans*, but through letters such as those of Cicero to Trebatius and Paetus.

The second immediate barrier is raised by a trait in Cicero's own character. Disraeli once remarked of Greville, the author of the Memoirs: 'He was the most conceited person with whom I have ever been brought in contact, though I have read Cicero and known Bulwer Lytton.' Even in contemporary Rome Cicero's conceit—which should more properly be called vanity—soon became notorious. In the year after his consulship we find him telling Metellus, a haughty noble, how a ripple of laughter had gone round the Senate when he confessed to his disappointment at not having been praised in a speech Metellus had made. For twenty more years, the Romans were to have the memory of that consulship kept green in season and out, in prose and in verse, in Latin and in Greek, by the ex-consul himself. His desire for public recognition was increased by his exile, after which he seems to have felt that only the voting of a Triumph for him could heal that wound to his vanity and his sense of justice. But it would be a hopeless task to try to palliate every instance of his touchiness. When Atticus wrote to him, 'Dionysius, an excellent fellow, as I too have found, a good scholar and devoted to you, arrived in Rome on December 16 and gave me your letter,' Cicero complained, 'You did not add "and he expressed his gratitude to you".' Imagine his indignation when his reprobate nephew began a sentence in a letter to him, 'Whatever can be said to your discredit, I . . . '!

If one is going to enjoy the letters, one must make up one's mind to be amused rather than exasperated by this constant itch for applause and appreciation. It is only one symptom of what I feel to be the determining element in Cicero's character—his dependence for his peace of mind on the good opinion of others. There is a tag from Homer that is always on his lips: 'I fear the reproach of the Trojans.' 'Think what I must be suffering', he bursts out to Atticus, 'when I am considered mad if I say what is right about politics, servile if I say what is expedient, crushed and helpless if I say nothing.' As a 'new man' with ambitions he had felt that his only chance of success and happiness was to adapt himself to the ways of the aristocracy to which his talents had obtained him entry. This attitude of mind had become habitual by the time the final rift appeared in the Roman State. No wonder he vacillated, when the people to whom he had assimilated himself were now taking sides against one another, and there were men in each camp to whose opinion he was sensitive!

But this sensitivity had its good results as well. On arriving in Asia Minor as Governor of Cilicia he was eager to win golden opinions. 'You will see', he wrote to Atticus, 'that the professions of a lifetime are now being put to the test. I hope I shall employ the training I have had from you and satisfy everybody.' He was just as anxious to satisfy the provincials as the Romans. Sometimes he was kept straight by the fear of being openly inconsistent with the high principles advocated in his philosophic works: 'I have bound myself to good conduct with six volumes for bail' (his recently published *Republic*). Once he goes further: 'What would History be saying of me a thousand years hence? That is a thing I fear much more than the petty gossip of those who are alive today.'

Another result of this dependence on others was a tendency to hero-worship. In his consulship Cicero did take the lead, bolstered up by the Senate and the Knights; but it was not long before he was feeling for the more congenial role of adviser to a natural leader; and even when he could no longer idealise Pompey himself, he continued to idealise his conception of what his relationship to Pompey might have been. Once again, in the last year of his life, he emerged for a few months as a leader, only to fall back soon into his instinctive role of would-be adviser to another natural leader. It is tragic to find him, at the end of a life which he believed devoted to freedom, justly reproached by Brutus with sacrificing the principles of freedom to his enthusiasm for the nineteen-year-old boy who was to become the emperor Augustus: 'It were better not to live than to live by his kind permission.'

A pupil of mine, set to write an essay on Cicero's political career, turned for inspiration to the *Encyclopaedia Britannica* and lighted by mistake on an entry that was suggestive, if irrelevant: 'CICERO, a town in Cook County (Ill.) bounded on the north, east and south by Chicago.' It is only too true: this fundamentally decent, respectable burgher of a small town found himself hemmed in on almost every side by politicians whom he realised too late to be gangster bosses. The only other side was bounded by a residential quarter of hereditary snobs.

But the vacillations of Cicero were increased by causes more creditable than a desire to please everybody. As a lawyer he was trained to extract principles from tangles of detail; and as an advocate he was trained to see what arguments could be adduced on each side. This made it particularly hard for him to make up his mind. I have heard, though the story may be only *ben trovato*, that when difficult issues presented themselves to the Baldwin Cabinet, Sir John Simon would write down the arguments on each side and then pass them over for Lord Halifax to make the decision.

A more serious complaint, the burden of Petrarch's first open letter, is that Cicero did not practise what he preached. It is undeniable that he did not always live up to the high principles enunciated in his philosophic works, even though he occasionally remembered them just in time. Everyone is pleased when a moralist is caught out, and Cicero is so unguarded in his letters that he is easy game. The oratorical education fashionable at Rome led both speakers and hearers, writers and readers, to assume that words need not be expected to correspond with facts. They took pleasure in effective advocacy for its own sake, without realising how easily this might encourage a general atmosphere of insincerity and hypocrisy. Again, the polite insincerities that serve the ends of social intercourse are apt to sound shocking when we meet them in Cicero's letters expressed in the fulsome superlatives which come so readily to the oratorical Italian.

I am not concerned, however, to reassess Cicero's character here: that would take a whole book, even if it were needed, and others whom I mentioned in the Preface have done him full justice. Whatever his faults, he was good company, he was on the side of conciliation, he was liberal and humane:—indeed he nearly humanised the Church before theology became aware of the danger. But what I want to stress rather is the perennial interest of the letters. It is easy to select from them only those that have 'human interest' and which require no special knowledge of the times; but that is to renounce a far deeper pleasure that can be had for a little trouble. It so happened that the life of Cicero coincided with one of those tides in the affairs of men when the cross-currents come to the surface so that we seem to see more clearly than usual the pattern of cause and effect. We recognise similar conjunctions when they occur again, and are tempted to evolve hazardous theories of historical cycles. We must beware indeed of seeing history through modern spectacles; and yet it is precisely the the recognition of analogous situations that makes such periods particularly exciting. The fall of the Roman Republic is a drama that has been re-enacted on all too many stages in our own generation; for beneath the transient rivalries of Pompeians and Caesarians, Republicans and Triumvirs, runs the recurrent plot of the dilemma between inefficient freedom and efficient dictatorship; and however much modern scholars may play down the ideological element, Cicero himself, though perplexed and misled by the many accidental complications, returned again and again to the belief that this was the fundamental issue. Of course the nobles were not good Social Democrats, and Caesar was a greater man than any Fascist dictator; but free speech at least is a fundamental right in any age, and it is none the less inhibited when the possible penalties are left to the imagination.

Cicero himself, trained, as I have said, to reduce complex issues to general principles, often does our work for us. There is a remarkable letter, written *de profundis* at the beginning of the Civil War, in which he tells Atticus that, to keep himself from breaking down completely, he is setting himself what we should call essay-questions on the present crisis. He lists some of these in Greek:

Should one remain in one's country even under a tyranny?

Are all means justifiable to abolish a tyranny, even if there is danger of ruining the State?

Should one take precautions to prevent the tyrannicide becoming tyrant himself?

Should one, if one's country is under a tyranny, try to help it by words and biding one's time, or by war?

Is one doing one's duty if one retires to some other place and remains there so long as one's country is under a tyranny, or should one brave any danger for the sake of liberation?

Should one invade one's country, or blockade it, if it is under a tyranny?

Should one enrol oneself in the ranks of the loyalists, even if one does not oneself approve of war as a means of abolishing tyranny?

Should one in public matters share the dangers of one's benefactors and friends, even if one believes their fundamental policy to be mistaken?

Should a man who has done great service to his country, and who has for that very reason incurred envy and injury, go out of his way to run risks for it, or should he be permitted eventually to take thought for himself and his loved ones, abandoning endless struggles against those who have the power?

The last of these questions is a *cri du cœur* of Cicero's own; but the others are all familiar stations on the *Via Dolorosa* of modern Europe.

It is essential then, if one is going to get the most out of the letters, to take the trouble to follow the political developments at least in outline. But there is a wealth of interesting and picturesque detail, both public and private, to enliven the journey. There are revealing sidelights on character: 'My reader Sositheus, a delightful fellow, has died, and I am more upset than perhaps I ought to be over the death of a slave;' 'When I write to you praising any of your friends, I should be grateful if you would let him know that I have done so;' 'Now that Tyrannio has arranged my books, my house seems to have acquired a soul;' 'I did not speak a word at the trial because my poor little girl, who is ill, was afraid I would provoke Clodius.' One remark to Atticus is particularly interesting: 'If this idea you favour of my seeking a Triumph had never entered my head, I should not come far short of the ideal statesman I sketched in Book VI of my *Republic*. . . . One cannot play both parts at once, the time-serving candidate for a Triumph and the independent politician. But do not doubt that I shall take honesty to be the best policy.'

Occasionally there is a dash of cynicism. 'I see Dolabella has been left a ninth of Livia's estate on condition he changes his name. Good essay-question in social ethics: "Should a young noble change his name in order to benefit under a lady's will?" We shall be able to answer it with more scientific accuracy when we know how much a ninth amounts to.' This cynicism, or perhaps one should call it flippancy, is particularly refreshing when applied to his own oratory. On one occasion Crassus found it expedient to praise Cicero's consul-ship. Cicero tells Atticus about it: 'He worked up pretty powerfully all that theme I often elaborate with variations in those speeches you are so hard on, all about fire and the sword (you know my purple patch) . . . When it came to my turn, Heavens how I showed off my paces in front of my new audience Pompey! Then if ever my rounded periods, my subtle transitions, my logical tricks and turns, stood me in good stead. Loud applause! No wonder, for the gist of it was the importance of the Senate, co-operation with the Knights, national unity, the paralysed remnants of the conspiracy, peace and plenty. You know how I can thunder on about all that. I need not tell you more: it was so loud you probably heard it over there in Greece.'

Cicero was not averse from a spot of gossip. When he was Governor of Cilicia Caelius wrote to him: 'There is no news at all, unless you want me to write you such gossip as this—and of course you do! . . . Paulla Valeria, the sister of Triarius, has divorced her husband without giving a reason, on the very day he was due back from his province. She's going to marry Decimus Brutus. She has sent back all her wardrobe. . . . Servius Galba would never have persuaded anyone he was an adulterer if he hadn't been caught in the act twice in three days. Where? In the last place I should have wished. But I leave it to you to worm it out of others. I rather like the idea of a victorious proconsul going round asking everyone in turn who the lady was with whom someone was caught.' But the traffic in gossip was not all one-way. While travelling in the heart of Asia Minor Cicero met one Vedius on the road with two two-wheeled and one four-wheeled carriage and horses, a litter, and a large following, including some wild asses and a dog-faced baboon in a cart. Shortly afterwards Vedius left his baggage temporarily with his host at Laodicea. During his absence his host died and the executor opened the baggage in error. In it he found five miniature busts of Roman ladies, one being of Brutus' sister, Junia. Cicero says he wanted to tell Atticus this by the way, 'since we are both pretty good gossips'. When he himself was looking round for a second wife he told Atticus he was not considering Pompey's daughter at present: 'As for the other you wrote about, I suppose you know her: I've never seen anything uglier.' Particularly interesting is his disquisition to Paetus, unfortunately untranslatable, on the Stoic idea that there is no such thing as obscenity of language (*Ad Fam.*, IX, 22). He quotes with gusto examples that prove the absurdity of conventional ideas on the subject, while professing to be himself on the side of Plato and modesty.

Cicero was, like Atticus, a keen art-collector. We find him disposing to a dealer of some unsuitable statues bought for him by an over-zealous friend. Where should he have put the Bacchantes, beautiful little figures though they are? The Muses would have done perhaps, if they had not been so expensive. But the Mars! What good was that to an advocate of peace? Anyway, pictures are what he really likes. On the other hand when Atticus found him at Athens some figures of Hermes in Pentelic marble for his 'Gymnasium' courtyard, he wrote at once: 'The more the merrier. I am so keen on these things that I expect you to help and others to disapprove. If none of Lentulus' ships is sailing, load them on any ship you like.' At the same time he wants some bas-reliefs to insert in the stucco walls of his hall, and two carved well-covers.

Atticus, among all his other activities, was a pioneer of publishing at Rome. There was no law of copyright, but a man with a good team of highly trained copyists could get hold of a manuscript and produce a complete edition before anyone else had access to it. Atticus made a regular business of this, and published all Cicero's works as well as those of other prominent Romans. We find Cicero taking him to task for letting Balbus have an advance copy of Book v of his *On Aims*, which in any case now required emendation, before he had sent one to Brutus to whom, at Atticus' own instigation, the work was dedicated. Another time he complains that Caerellia, a lady who was a close friend of his, is prematurely circulating copies of the same work: his own master-copy has never been out of his sight, so she must have had access to those in the hands of Atticus' copyists; but he cannot blame them, as he forgot to tell them he wanted publication delayed.

Atticus was not only publisher, but reader and adviser. On one occasion he suggested a nautical metaphor, *inhibere*, to render the Greek work for philosophic suspense of judgement. Cicero replied: 'At first your suggestion attracted me very much, but now I strongly disapprove of it . . . I thought rowers rested on their oars when told *inhibere*, but yesterday, when a ship put in near my house, I discovered it was not so. They don't rest on their oars: they *back water*.'

Our own island comes into the story. Cicero was much interested in Caesar's invasion of 54 B.C., and wrote to his brother: 'The outcome of the campaign in Britain is anxiously awaited; for everyone knows that the approaches to the island are walled with astonishing cliffs. It has also been ascertained that there is not a scrap of silver in the island, nor any hope of booty except slaves; and I don't think you can expect any of those to have had a literary or musical education.' Shortly afterwards Caesar wrote to him from near Dover. Britain had been settled; hostages had been taken but no booty, and a tribute imposed. The army was now being withdrawn. (This letter took twenty-seven days to reach him.)

None of the examples I have given to illustrate the diversity of the correspondence is from letters included in the selection that follows. I hope they may have aroused the curiosity of any reader who has got so far, and tempted him (or her) to persevere.

# Note

ON

*Les Secrets de la Correspondance de Cicéron*

BY

Jerôme Carcopino. 2 Vols. Paris, 1947

The publication of this learned and ingenious work, sensational though it is in some respects, would not call for comment in a book such as this, had not its conclusions been swallowed whole by the reviewer in at least one of our national weeklies.

Volume I is an unrelieved indictment of Cicero, who emerges as a social, financial and political crook, a weak-kneed counterpart of Pierre Laval. Many of his faults are indeed plain to see, and still more reveal themselves when facts from outside sources are adduced, or when one letter is set against another. But M. Carcopino's method is never to give Cicero the benefit of any doubt, and seldom (despite disclaimers) to allow for differences of standard between our own age and the first century B.C. Moreover the modern standards applied are those of a prosecuting barrister.

Gaston Boissier, in his admirable *Cicéron et ses amis*, first published in 1865, prophesied sadly: 'One of these days a prying commentator will study these too unreserved disclosures, and will use them to draw a portrait to scare posterity of the indiscreet person who made them. He will prove by exact and irrefutable quotation that he was a bad citizen and a bad friend, that he loved neither his country nor his family, that he was jealous of honest people, and that he betrayed all parties. It is not so, however, and a wise man will not be deceived by the artifice of misleading quotations.'

Volume II develops a startling new theory. The letters have now been shown to be so damning in their total effect that they must have been selected and published at the instigation of an enemy on purpose to blacken Cicero's memory. Who had the motive and the necessary influence? The 'crafty tyrant' of Gibbon, of course—the future Augustus. The publication of the letters was part of his propaganda campaign before the Battle of Actium (34–32 B.C.). All his enemies, past and present, would come out badly, and his adoptive father, Caesar, would come out well. As accomplices he must have had Cicero's unworthy friend Atticus and his unworthy son Marcus, both of them anxious to curry favour.

However ingeniously the arguments for this theory are worked out (and this is not the place to consider them in detail), it seems incredible as soon as we disentangle ourselves from the trees and look round again at the wood. Seventy years ago Strachan-Davidson summed up his feelings about Cicero thus: 'He is one of those characters whose faults lie on the surface; and the preservation of his most secret letters has withdrawn the veil which hides the weakness and pettiness of most men from the eyes of posterity. His memory has thus been subjected to a test of unprecedented sharpness. Nevertheless, the faithful friends who resolved to present to the world his confidential utterances, unspoiled by editorial garbling, have not only earned our gratitude by the gift of a unique historical monument, but have judged most nobly and most truly what was due to the reputation of Cicero. As it was in his lifetime, so it has been with his memory; those who have known him most intimately have commonly loved him best. He is no demi-god to be set on a pedestal for the worship of the nations, but a man with human virtues and human weaknesses, and withal possessed of a charm of grace and goodness which makes us think of him as of some familiar and beloved friend.' These words of a Victorian don may err on the side of indulgence; but does not the fact that the letters can make such an impression on a reasonable and civilised man rule out the idea that they were published in malice, or that their publication could serve the ends of an enemy as practical as the future Augustus?[1]

Most of those who read all through the letters seem to emerge with a soft spot for Cicero, however often he may have let them down. Nothing has happened in the past hundred years to make us revise appreciably the balanced, humane and penetrating judgements of Boissier, a critic worthy of the country of Sainte-Beuve.

1. For some arguments against Carcopino, see D. R. Shackleton Bailey's edition of the Letters to Atticus, Vol 1, pp. 61–75.

# Prologue

## 106 to 63 B.C.

Marcus Tullius Cicero was born in 106 B.C. at Arpinum (now Arpino), a hill-town near Cassino. His family belonged to the powerful class of well-to-do men of affairs known as the Knights, which ranked next after the Roman Senate and rivalled it in influence. The period of his boyhood was dominated by another man from Arpino, Gaius Marius, the great soldier who reorganised the Roman Army and saved Italy from the Germanic hordes, but incidentally paved the way for dictatorship. Marcus, with his young brother Quintus, was sent to Rome for his education in rhetoric, philosophy and law. By the time he was ready to enter public life a horrible civil war had replaced Marius, the champion of the People's Party (those politicians who sought power through the popular assembly), by another great soldier, Sulla, the champion of the Senatorial Party (which centred round the 'nobles'). At the age of twenty-six he came to the fore with a courageous speech in defence of a man wrongfully accused by one of Sulla's most notorious agents. This brought him considerable popularity; but in 79, partly for reasons of security and of health, he went abroad. At Athens he cemented his lifelong friendship with Titus Pomponius Atticus, who lived mainly there or at Butrinto on the coast of N.W. Greece opposite Corfu. Atticus was a Knight in status and an Epicurean in philosophy; he made a point of keeping in with everyone.

At Rhodes Cicero perfected his oratory, public speaking being the chief road to political success. After his return he was in 76 elected to the quaestorship, the first rung of the fourfold ladder of high offices—

quaestor, aedile, praetor, consul.[1] Thus a 'new man', whose loyalty
had been to his own order, the Knights, obtained life membership of
the Senate. Conciliation was always his policy, and, with his advance-
ment, it became his ideal to promote the 'Concord of the Orders',
Senate and Knights, as the only safeguard against civil war (for despite
his natural admiration for Marius of Arpino, he had no use for the
People's Party). He had married the capable and ambitious Terentia,
who bore him, in 76, a beloved daughter Tullia, and about twelve
years later a son, Marcus. In 68 he inherited the family home at Arpino
and acquired his suburban residence at Tusculum, on the ridge above
Frascati. He also bought houses at various places in Southern Italy—
Anzio, Pompeii, Pozzuoli, etc.— such as any person of substance had
in an age when inns were primitive.

We must now take stock of the political situation at Rome in the
middle sixties, when the extant correspondence of Cicero begins. The
power of the Senatorial Party, restored by Sulla, had begun to decline.
In 70 they had broken with Sulla's successor as the most powerful man
in Rome, Gnaeus Pompey, already surnamed 'the Great'. As consul
Pompey got a bill passed taking from them two-thirds of the all-
important seats on the juries; one-third went to the Knights, and one-
third to the class next to them in wealth. He thus won the favour of the
Knights, and when, after clearing the Eastern Mediterranean of pirates,
he was proposed, in 66, as supreme commander in Asia Minor, where
the Empire still seemed threatened by King Mithridates of Pontus,
the Knights and People's Party united to support him. Cicero spoke
warmly for him on this occasion, and long cherished the hope that he
would prove a leader such as the younger Scipio had been in the
previous century, fit to preside over his 'Concord of the Orders'.

The head of the Knights was Crassus, the richest man in Rome, an
unscrupulous financier who traded on the fact that so many people
owed him money. The rising hope of the People's Party was a noble a
few years younger than Cicero and Pompey, Julius Caesar, the nephew
of Marius. He was in financial embarrassments, however, and was not
yet thought of as the equal of Pompey.

1. The twenty quaestors were paymasters; the four aediles were superin-
tendents of public places and the activities that took place in them; the eight
praetors were the chief judicial magistrates; the two consuls were the joint heads
of the Roman Republic. Election was in each case for one year only.

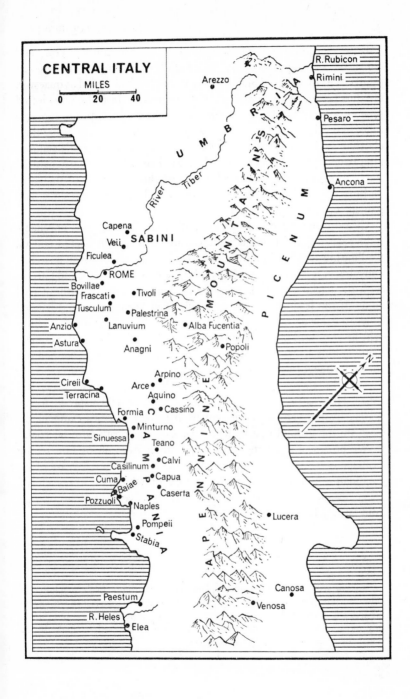

CENTRAL ITALY

MILES
0 20 40

In 70 Cicero had been elected aedile for the coming year, and enhanced his reputation by successfully prosecuting Verres, an oppressive Governor of Sicily, where he himself had served as quaestor. He thus became early a champion of provincials. In 67 he was elected praetor, and in 64 he was a candidate for the consulship, the supreme office in the State, held jointly by two men for the year succeeding their election. Atticus seems to have come to Rome at his friend's request, after twenty years' residence in Greece, to help win over the Senatorial Party to support the 'new man' in his candidature. One of the competitors was Catiline, a bankrupt noble who had turned extremist and gained support from others in a like situation.

Cicero came out on top of the poll, with Antonius, an unreliable noble, second, and Catiline a close third. In 63, with Cicero consul, Catiline mustered various discontented elements in Italy for an anarchist conspiracy. A 'state of emergency' was thereupon declared, and Cicero, with the backing of a majority in the Senate, executed without trial some of the leading conspirators, who had been caught red-handed in treasonable acts. By taking this responsibility, at great risk to himself, he may well have saved the State, as he ever afterwards claimed. Catiline himself was soon killed in the battle that finally stamped out the conspiracy. In this crisis the Knights had stood by Cicero and the Senate. But there was an ominous incident when he laid down his office. He was prevented from making the customary speech to the people by the veto of a tribune[1] fresh from Pompey's camp in the East, on the ground that he had put citizens to death without trial.

We possess a few letters of Cicero dating from 68–65 but, owing principally to Atticus' presence in Rome, none from the years of his candidature and consulship, the history of which we know chiefly from his speeches. From now onwards, however, the story may be told largely from his own letters.

---

1. The tribunes, ten in number, were by origin the people's watchdogs to offset the power of the Senatorial executive. As they were each armed with a veto whereby they could check the magistrates' acts or proposals, they could prevent any measure from being ratified. They had come to be used as agents by the Senate or by factions in the game of politics.

# I

# 62 to 58 B.C.

*Pompey, due back from the East after defeating Mithridates, was apparently displeased at Cicero's stealing the limelight, and ignored a long account he sent of his suppression of Catiline's conspiracy. Our first letter expresses Cicero's disappointment. It failed to penetrate Pompey's reserve, but, in spite of annoyance freely expressed to Atticus, Cicero continued to base his hopes on him. For Pompey had now shown evidence of constitutional intentions by disbanding his army on his return to Italy at the end of 62.*

*We may be more tolerant of Cicero's continual praises of his own consulship if we remember that, unless it were admitted that he had saved the State, he had no defence against the charge that continually hung over him of putting citizens to death illegally. His mistake was to insist too much. At least he had restored the prestige of the Senate, and shown that in a crisis the 'Concord of the Orders' could be a reality.*

*To Pompey, in Asia Minor*        *Rome, Summer, 62 B.C.*

I trust all is well with you and your army.

Your official despatch gave extreme pleasure to all, and to me in particular. It held out high hopes of peace such as I have always promised to everyone from my complete confidence in you. But I must also tell you that your old enemies, lately turned friends,[1] were completely shattered by it, and lie prostrate amid the ruins of their great expectations.

1. Presumably Caesar and the People's Party, who had been making overtures to Pompey.

As for your private letter to me, although it contained only a meagre expression of your personal regard, I assure you it was welcome; for nothing gives me more pleasure than the consciousness of having done well by others, and if ever I get less than my share in return, I am quite content that the balance of services rendered should rest with me. And I have no doubt that, even if my great zeal on your behalf has not fully succeeded in winning your attachment, the interests of the State will effect and cement our union.

Still, to make it quite clear what I missed in your letter, I will write frankly, as my own nature and our friendship demands. I have lately achieved things which led me to expect, both on the score of our intimacy and of their importance for the State, some word of congratulation in a letter from you; and I conceive that you only left it out for fear of offending someone. So let me tell you that what I did for the safety of the State has been ratified by the considered approval of the whole world; and when you come home you will realise that I acted with such wisdom and courage that (since, while you are much greater than Scipio was, I am not much inferior to his Laelius,[1]) you will readily allow me to associate with you both in politics and in private life.                                                              (*Ad Fam.*, v, 7)

*To Sestius, in Macedonia*                        *Rome, December*, 62 B.C.
... Spurred on by your message of some time ago congratulating me on having bought a house from Crassus and wishing me good luck with it, I have now justified you in retrospect by buying it, for 3500 sestertia.[2] So I have to tell you that I am now so heavily in debt that I am eager to join a conspiracy if anyone will have me; but while some blackball me out of hatred, open hatred for my having crushed the other conspiracy, others distrust me and think I am setting a trap, not believing that the man who rescued the bankers from blockade can himself be short of cash! As a matter of fact there is plenty of money

1. The philosophic friend and mentor of the younger Scipio in the previous century.
2. A large sum. It is pointless to give supposed English equivalents where the only thing relevant is purchasing power, which is hard to determine and varies so quickly. The house was on the fashionable Palatine Hill.

to be had at 6 per cent; and my exploits as consul have at least had the result that I am considered a good security. . . .

(Ad Fam., v, 6, 2)

*To Atticus, in N.W. Greece*                    *Rome, January* 25, 61 B.C.

. . . I expect you have heard that when the women's sacrifice to the Good Goddess was taking place in Caesar's house, a man in woman's clothes got in;[1] and that after the Vestal Virgins[2] had performed the sacrifice afresh, the matter was brought up in the Senate by Cornificius (he was the instigator, please note, and not one of us ex-consuls). A motion was then passed referring the case to the Vestals and the Pontifical College, and they pronounced it sacrilege. Thereupon the consuls were requested by the Senate to set up a court of inquiry. Caesar meanwhile divorced his wife.[3] Piso the consul, out of friendship for Clodius, is doing everything he can to get this proposal turned down, though he is himself its sponsor, and that by order of the Senate —in a matter of sacrilege too! Messala, the other consul, is so far taking a very severe line. The Right, at Clodius' urgent request, are keeping clear of the whole affair; gangs are being collected; I myself, who at first showed a Draconian severity, am daily cooling down, but Cato is still pressing the matter energetically. To cut a long story short, I'm afraid this lack of interest from the respectable, and warm support from the disreputable, may lead to much political trouble.

Your friend (you know who I mean?) the man of whom you wrote that he began to praise me as soon as he feared to disparage me,[4] ostensibly loves me, is devoted to me, adores me, heaps me with praises; inwardly (though one can see through him) he is jealous. He has no graciousness, no straightforwardness, no principles in politics, no glamour or strength or generosity. But I will write to you about all this in more detail another time: so far I have not got to the bottom of it, and I dare not entrust a letter on such important topics to this Tom, Dick or Harry of a messenger, . . .     (*Ad Att.*, 1, 13, 3–4)

1. A dissolute young noble named Clodius Pulcher, who had espoused the People's Party. He became a leading gangster whom only Caesar could control.
2. The priestesses of Vesta. The sacrifice was taking place in Caesar's house. It was held in the house of a magistrate with *imperium*, and he was City Praetor.
3. The occasion of his famous dictum 'Caesar's wife must be above suspicion'. This was his second wife, Pompeia.
4. Pompey.

*To Atticus, in N.W. Greece*                              *Rome, June,* 61 B.C.

... If you want to know about Clodius' trial, the result was incredible; so much so that now after the event everyone has come round to my opinion and blames Hortensius. The challenging of the jurymen took place amid an uproar, since the prosecutor like a good censor rejected all the bad characters, while the defendant like a kind-hearted collector of gladiators refused all the most respectable; so as soon as the jury took their seats, decent people began to have grave misgivings. You never saw such a disreputable crew even in a cabaret dive: senators with a black mark, knights without a penny, treasury officials in the role of treasure-hunters. There were still among them a few honest men whom Clodius had not managed to eliminate; these sat there glum and gloomy like fish out of water, much upset at finding themselves in contact with such dirt.

At the preliminary proceedings, as point after point was put before the jury, their show of rectitude and unanimity was remarkable. The defendant did not gain a point, while the prosecution were allowed even more than they asked for. Hortensius, naturally, was beginning to be jubilant over his perspicacity; everyone there regarded Clodius not as accused, but rather as condemned already a thousand times. You probably heard the noise over there, when I entered the witness-box and his supporters began to hoot; but the jury sprang to my defence and openly offered to sacrifice their own necks to save mine. This seemed to me an even greater compliment than your fellow-Athenians paid Xenocrates when they refused to let him be sworn before giving evidence, or our Roman jury paid Metellus Numidicus when they would not look at the accounts which he submitted according to the normal procedure. Yes, a much greater compliment. The shouts of the jury, defending me as 'Saviour of the country' crushed the defendant, and his supporters collapsed with him; and on the next day my crowd of callers was as great as that which escorted me home when I retired from my consulship. . . . No one thought Clodius would defend his case.

Tell me now, ye Muses, how first the fire fell.

You know who I mean by Baldhead,[1] my trumpet-blower, whose

1. Crassus, now in league with Caesar and the People's Party.

complimentary speech about me I mentioned to you. Well, he fixed up the whole job in a couple of days with the help of a slave, and a gladiator at that. He sent for people, gave promises, sureties, cash down. He even went so far—God, what a scandal!—as to enhance the bribe to some members of the jury by offering nights with certain ladies and introductions to young men of good family. Those who had any decency withdrew wholesale; yet although the Forum[1] was packed with slaves, there were still twenty-five jurymen who had the courage to risk their necks, preferring to ruin themselves rather than their country. But thirty-one there were who thought more about poverty than probity. . . .                                   (*Ad Att.*, 1, 16, 3–5)

*Part of the Senate, led by the rigid Cato, had seen in this escapade a chance of suppressing the renegade Clodius. Cicero, despite his early inclination to keep aloof, intervened to destroy Clodius' alibi, and thereby made a mortal enemy with momentous consequences to himself.*

*Meanwhile the outlook for Cicero's 'Concord of the Orders' was black. The Knights were estranged because the Senate refused to revise the terms of a contract for levying the taxes on Asia Minor, over which they had lost heavily. On the other hand Pompey was annoyed because the Senate, poorly requiting his overtures and his good faith in disbanding his army, refused to ratify* en bloc *his settlement of Eastern problems or to provide for grants of land to his ex-servicemen, though Cicero advised them to do so.*

*From 61 to the middle of 58 Cicero badly missed the help of his brother, who went to be Governor of West Asia Minor.*

*To Atticus, in N.W. Greece*                    Rome, January 20, 60 B.C.
    I must say, there is nothing I miss so much at the moment as a man with whom I can share all my worries, who is fond of me and sensible, to whom I can speak without any pretence or reserve or concealment. My brother, so straightforward and affectionate, is away. Camillus (?) suggests not a human being but

    1. The main square of Rome which, with the surrounding buildings, was the centre of both political and legal activity.

Sands and shores and desert wildernesses.

And as for you, who have so often relieved my anxiety and depression
by your talk and advice, who are my constant ally in public affairs,
my confidant in private, my partner in every conversation and project,
where on earth are you? I am so utterly forlorn that the only peaceful
hours I have are those spent with my wife, my little daughter and my
darling boy. For my spectacular put-on friendships with the great,
though they are not without glamour in the big world, give me no
enjoyment in private. Thus when my house is well filled with callers
in the morning, and I go down to the Forum surrounded with troops
of friends, I cannot find in all that crowd a single soul with whom I
can exchange either an unguarded joke or an intimate grumble. So it is
you I'm waiting for, you I'm longing for; in fact you must come. I
have many worries and anxieties which I feel could be dissipated in a
single walk and talk, if only I could have your ear.

All the pinpricks and sores of my private troubles I will leave
undisclosed, and will not commit them to a letter carried by an unknown messenger. True, they are not over-serious—I should not like
you to get alarmed; but they are always there, and give me no peace,
and I have no sympathetic friend to relieve them with talk and advice.
As for the body politic, the spirit is willing, but again and again the
very remedies applied open fresh wounds. If I were to give you a
summary of what has happened since you left, you would exclaim that
it is impossible for the State of Rome to stand a day longer. After you
left, I think, the first thing that came on the scene was the Clodian
drama. There I thought I saw a chance of using the surgeon's knife
on immorality and curbing youthful excesses; I blew hot and strong
and used all the resources of my mind and powers, not out of hatred
for anyone, but in the hope not so much of castigating as curing the
body politic. But a great blow has been dealt the State through the
corruption and debauching of the jury. Now observe the sequel. We
have had a consul thrust upon us whom nobody less philosophic than
ourselves can look at without groaning. Was this a serious blow? Yes.
Though the Senate passed a motion about bribery and about juries,
nothing has been made law; the Senate has been frightened out of it,
and the Knights estranged. So a single year has overturned the two

bulwarks of the State whose establishment was my particular service: it has thrown away the prestige of the Senate and broken up the harmony of the two Orders. . . .

Meanwhile there is not a ghost of a statesman in sight. The man who could be one, my friend Pompey (for such he is, I would have you know), safeguards by silence the triumphal cloak awarded him. Crassus never utters a word that could make him unpopular. The rest you know well enough: such fools, that they seem to think they can let the country go to rack and ruin and still keep their precious fishponds safe. There only is one who does anything about it, more I think by his firmness and integrity than by his judgement and ability—Cato: and he has now for nearly three months been worrying the wretched tax-collectors, with whom he used to be so popular, and won't let the Senate give them an answer. So we are obliged to shelve all other decrees until they are answered. And for the same reason I suppose even the usual reception of foreign delegations will have to be put off. . . .                                   (*Ad Att.*, I, 18, 1–3; 6–7)

*To Atticus, in Greece*                              *Rome, June,* 60 B.C.

. . . You ask me why I am urging you to come, and at the same time indicate that you are involved in business affairs; but you say you are ready to hurry over not only if it is necessary, but if I should like it. Well, I cannot say it is really necessary, but I did think you might arrange your various periods abroad more conveniently. You stay away too long, especially as you are not far off, so that I can't enjoy your company, and you lack mine. At the moment there is a lull, but at the slightest sign of progress in the mad designs of our little Beauty[1] I shall jolly well hound you out of your retreat! But Metellus keeps him in check splendidly, and will continue to do so. He is proving, by the way, a most patriotic consul, and sound at heart as I have always thought him.

Clodius is not merely pretending, but openly aiming at becoming a tribune of the plebeians. When the matter was discussed in the Senate I crushed the fellow and accused him of inconsistency in that he was seeking the tribunate at Rome whereas in Sicily he had constantly declared that it was an inheritance he was seeking; I added that we

1. Clodius, whose other name was Pulcher (= beautiful).

need not worry much, since he would no more be allowed to ruin the country as a plebeian[1] than patricians like him had been allowed in my consulship . . . In fact I am sobering his insolence not only by regular speeches but by repartee. So even I twit him in casual conversation and make fun of him. Thus when recently we were escorting a friend who was standing for office he asked me whether I had been in the habit of giving my protégés the Sicilians seats for the gladiatorial shows. I said, no. 'Well then,' said he, 'as their new patron I will start the practice; though my sister, with all the space reserved for the consul at her disposal, will hardly allow me a foot.' 'Don't reproach her with denying you a foot,' I said, 'seeing that she puts more than that at your disposal.'[2] Hardly a joke for an ex-consul to make, you will say. I admit it, but she's a disgrace to the consulship, and I hate her.

> She wages civil war—against her husband,

and not only against Metellus, but against Fabius[3] . . .

You asked about the Land Bill: I must say it seems to be a frost by now. You also gave me a gentle rap over the knuckles for my intimacy with Pompey, but please don't think that it is to secure my own safety that I have thrown in my lot with him: the position is, that if any disagreement should arise between us, the State would be involved in a wholesale rupture. Against this I have taken precautions, and so planned things that without falling away from my own ideal policy he should behave better and give up pandering to the popular whim. And I must say he speaks far more glowingly about my achievements than about his own, though many had urged him to decry them. He affirms that whereas he did well by the State, I preserved its existence. What good his conduct in this can do me I don't know, but I know it is good for the State. What if I can make a better citizen also of Caesar, who has the wind in his sails just now? Would this do the State such

1. To become a tribune Clodius (who pointedly used this low-class spelling of his great patrician name of Claudius) would have to get himself made a plebeian by adoption. By this time plebeians were often wealthy bourgeois and they could hold any office. The distinction between them and patricians counted for little.

2. Rumour accused Clodius of incest with his sister Clodia, the fascinating and notorious 'Lesbia' of the poet Catullus. She was married to the consul Metellus.

3. Perhaps one of her 'three-hundred' lovers.

harm? Besides, even if no one envied me and all supported me as they should, still a cure which healed the diseased portions of the body politic would be preferable to one which amputated them. As it is, when those Knights whom once I stationed on the slope of the Capitol[1] with you as their captain and standard-bearer have deserted the Senate, and when our leading senators think they are practically in heaven if they have bearded mullets in their fish-ponds that will come and feed out of their hand, and trouble about nothing else, don't you think I deserve some credit if I take from those who have the power the will to abuse it?

I am just as devoted to Cato as you are, but with the best intentions and from the highest principles he sometimes does the State harm. He talks as if he were living in Plato's Republic instead of on Romulus' dunghill. What could be fairer than that a man who takes a bribe as a juryman should himself be put in the dock? That was Cato's proposition, and the Senate agreed. Result—the Knights at odds with the Senate: not with me—I voted against it. Again, what could be more outrageous than for the tax-collectors to break their contract? Still, the right course was to put up with the loss for the sake of keeping the Knights' goodwill. Cato objected and won the day. Result—when a consul has been thrown into prison and riots have been a daily occurrence, no one of those whom I and my successors in the consulship used to rally round us in defence of the constitution has moved an eyelid. 'What?' you will say, 'must we then bribe these men like mercenaries?' How can we help it, if there's no alternative? Would you have us enslaved to freedmen and even slaves?

But, as you would say, enough of the *grand sérieux.* . . .

(Ad Att., I, I, 4–8)

*To Atticus, on his way home. In the country*        *? December,* 60 B.C.
 . . . In finding fault with the narrowness of my windows, let me tell you that you are finding fault with the Training of Cyrus.[2] For when I made the same remark to Cyrus, he replied that a view of a garden was not so pleasing through a wide window; for let *A* be the

---

1. The citadel of Rome, just behind the Forum. The occasion was when Cicero rallied the Knights against Catiline.
2. Cyrus was an architect. Cicero is playing on the title of Xenophon's famous work on the training of Cyrus who founded the Persian Empire.

point of vision, *B–C* the object, *D* etc. the rays—you see what follows. If it were true that our sight was due to the impact of images on the eyes, these would be terribly cramped in a narrow space; but as it is, the emission of rays goes on merrily enough.[1] If you have any other complaints, you will have to argue, unless it is something that could be put right without expense.

Now for January and my attitude and policy, as to which, following Socratic practice, I will put both sides of the question, but at the end, no less Socratically, give my own opinion. It certainly is a matter that takes some thinking out. Either (*a*) I must resist the Land Bill strongly, which would involve a certain amount of fighting but much increase my prestige, or (*b*) I must keep quiet, which means retiring to Solonium or Anzio, or (*c*) I must support it, which they say Caesar is quite convinced I shall do; for Cornelius came to see me—I mean Cornelius Balbus, Caesar's friend—and assured me that Caesar would consult Pompey and me about everything and would make an effort to reconcile Pompey and Crassus. In favour of (*c*) are the following advantages: intimate connections with Pompey, and with Caesar too, if I like; reconciliation with my enemies; peace with the masses; and a quiet old age. But I am moved by my own *finale* in Book III of my poem:

> The road which in your earliest years you chose,
> As consul too with steadfast courage trod,
> Keep to that road, add lustre to your fame,
> And give all patriots cause to bless your name.

Since the Muse Calliope herself dictated these words to me in a book full of noble and lordly utterances, I do not think I ought for a moment to reject the motto of Hector:

> There is no omen true but this, to stand
> And be a bulwark of your fatherland.

But let us keep all this for our walks during the Compitalia. Don't

---

1. The Epicureans believed that vision was due to the impact of images on the eye; Theophrastus (whom Cicero affects to believe), that it was due to rays sent out from the eye.

forget about the day before the holiday. I will have the bath-water heated and Terentia is inviting Pomponia; we will get your mother to come too. Please bring me Theophrastus on *The Pursuit of Preferment* from Quintus' library.                                      (*Ad Att.*, II, 3, 2–3)

*In the summer of 60 Caesar had returned from a successful campaign in Portugal, and stood for the consulship. The Senate could not prevent his election, but it refused to name for him an important governorship to follow his year of office. Thereupon he entered into a secret compact, known as the First Triumvirate, with Pompey, who was equally tired of Senatorial obstruction, and Crassus, who had the money. Pompey also married Caesar's daughter Julia. Cicero was invited to join, and seriously considered it; but much as he disliked and despised the nobles, his loyalty to the constitution eventually prevailed over his ambition. He realised that the Triumvirate meant un-Republican personal rule.*

*To satisfy Pompey, Caesar as consul in 59 brought in another Land Bill for the resettlement of his ex-servicemen. He rode roughshod over Senatorial opposition, and with open support from Pompey carried the Bill in the Popular Assembly, disregarding the veto of tribunes. This was a clear indication that the Triumvirs were not going to be held up by respect for the constitution. Twenty commissioners were appointed to administer the Bill.*

*Next Pompey's Eastern settlement was ratified; the tax-collecting Knights got a remission of one third of the contracted price; and Caesar, having thus satisfied his partners, obtained as his province for five years the Po valley (Hither Gaul), the Dalmatian area (Illyricum) and finally also Southern France (Further Gaul). It was this that enabled him to consolidate his power for the future.*

*Cicero meanwhile prudently took a holiday, but watched with growing anxiety the encroachments of the Triumvirs. His dilemma was this: he believed passionately in freedom (though it had been abused) and in constitutionalism (though the Senate was incompetent to govern the Empire); but he was attached to Pompey and flattered by Caesar, while the nobles did everything to alienate him.*

*To Atticus, at Rome*                                      *Anzio, April,* 59 B.C.
In my previous letter I promised that some work would emerge

from this tour of mine, but now I cannot be so sure. I've so fallen in love with leisure that I can't be torn away from it. So either I enjoy myself with my books, of which I have a splendid lot at Anzio, or I sit counting the waves, as the stormy weather is unsuitable for fishing. The thought of writing positively repels me. The work on geography which I had projected is a laborious business; Eratosthenes, my proposed source, is so strongly criticised by Serapion and Hipparchus. You can imagine the effect if Tyrannio also takes a hand. Besides, the subject is infernally hard to explain, and monotonous, and not so capable of embroidery as I thought.

But the chief thing is, that I snatch at any excuse for idleness. I even wonder whether I will not settle down at Anzio and spend the rest of this period here. Why, I would rather have been one of the two chief magistrats here than one of the consuls at Rome. You chose the better part and set up house at Butrinto; but believe me, the Anzians' community here is a good second. To think that there is a place so near Rome where there are plenty of people who have never seen Vatinius; where there is no one but me who cares whether any of Caesar's Twenty Commissioners is dead or alive; where no one intrudes upon me, but everyone is friendly! This is the one and only place to be a statesman. At Rome it has become not only impracticable but boring. So I will write a journal, for your own private consumption, in the style of Theopompus, or even much more bitter. I have no policy now, unless you count hating the Left; and even that I do with no rancour, but rather as a pleasant form of literary exercise. . . .

(*Ad Att.*, II, 6)

*To Atticus, on his way to N.W. Greece.*          *Rome, Summer,* 59 B.C.

I have had several letters from you, and understood from them your tense anxiety for any news. We are hemmed in on every side and no longer refuse to be slaves, but fear exile and death as if these were greater evils, though in fact they are much smaller. Yes, that is the state of affairs, and though everyone unites in deploring it, not a word is said to remedy it. The goal of the powers that be, it seems, is to leave nothing for anyone else to give away. The only voice raised, and that openly, is young Curio's. He is the recipient of loud applause, highly complimentary demonstrations, and countless other signs of goodwill from the constitutionalists, while Fufius is a target for hoots and hisses and general abuse. But this increases one's misery rather than one's hope, at observing how, while the people's will remains free, their courage is enslaved. You need not ask about minutiae; the whole situation has come to such a pass that there is no hope of even those in office, let alone private individuals, ever regaining their freedom. Yet despite this oppression speech is freer at any rate in social gatherings and over the dinner-table, than it was. Disgust is beginning to get the better of fear, without, however, alleviating the universal despair. The Campanian Land Bill too prescribes an oath to be taken at a public meeting by all candidates for office, binding themselves never to suggest any scheme for tenure of the land other than that embodied in Caesar's Law. No one hesitated to take it— except Laterensis, who is considered a hero for withdrawing his candidature for the tribuneship rather than comply.

But I have not the heart to write any more about politics. I am not at all pleased with myself, and it hurts me a great deal to write. I keep my end up, not discreditably considering the general servility, but not courageously considering my distinguished past. Caesar has most handsomely offered me a place on his personal staff, as his deputy, and I have also been offered a titular embassy.[1] But the latter would involve a far from safe trust in the tender mercies of our little Beauty,[2] as well as my absence at the time of my brother's return; the former provides better safeguards, and would not prevent me from being here if I chose. I am keeping the embassy up my sleeve, but doubt if I shall use it. But who knows? I don't want to run away: I am longing to fight it out. I have people's warm support. But I guarantee nothing, and please do not mention all this.

I am upset about Quintus' freeing his Statius and about other things; still I've become quite inured by now. I wish you were here—more than wish; then I should have advice and sympathy. But hold yourself in readiness to dash over if I call for you.     ( *Ad Att.*, II, 18)

*To Atticus, in N.W. Greece*                    *Rome, July,* 59 B.C.
   . . . Pompey, my favourite, to my infinite regret, has done himself irreparable harm. No one supports the Triumvirs out of good will,

---

1. Nominally to discharge a vow. It enabled a senator to travel outside Italy with ambassadorial privileges.
2. Clodius would then be able to prosecute him as a private citizen.

and I fear they may be driven to resort to force. I do not quarrel with
their side, owing to my old friendship with Pompey, but neither do I
give it my approval, for that would be to stultify all my previous
actions. I keep to the broad highroad. Public opinion can best be
discerned at the theatre and shows. At the gladiatorial show both the
master[1] and his supporters were torn to shreds with hisses. At the
Festival of Apollo the actor Diphilus made a vicious attack on our
Pompey the Great: the line

> Great thou art by our undoing

was encored a thousand times; the whole theatre rose at the passage

> Time will come when ye shall rue
> the very prowess that he showed,

and at what follows likewise. For those lines fit so well that you would
think they were topical verses written against Pompey by an enemy.
The speech beginning

> If nor law nor conscience rule thee

was received with tumultuous applause. When Caesar entered, the
applause died down; but young Curio, who followed, was applauded
as Pompey used to be in the good old constitutional days. Caesar is
much annoyed. Rumour has it that a letter has gone post haste to
Pompey at Capua. The Triumvirs are angry with the Knights for
standing up and applauding Curio, and ill-disposed to everyone. They
are threatening to repeal the Roscian Law, and even the Corn Law.[2]
Things certainly are boiling up. I should have preferred nothing to
be said about their policies, but now I am afraid that may prove impossible. People won't put up with it, yet it seems they will have to. There
is now complete unanimity, cemented by hatred but otherwise helpless.

Moreover our dear Clodius is constantly threatening me: he's an
enemy. Trouble is impending which will require your immediate

1. Pompey.
2. The former reserved fourteen rows at the theatre for the Knights, the
latter helped the common people by providing cheap corn.

presence. I fancy I can count absolutely on the ranks of all the loyalists, and even semi-loyalists, who rallied round me in my consulship. Pompey is displaying considerable goodwill towards me. He also declares that Clodius will not breathe a word against me—which he may believe, but I do not. Cosconius has died, and I have been asked to step into his shoes.[1] Dead man's shoes indeed! I should gain the worst possible reputation, and nothing could be less in accordance with your motto of 'Safety First'. For the Commission is unpopular with the loyalists, I with the disloyal. I should keep my own unpopularity and saddle myself with that of others as well. Caesar would like me join his staff. That would be a more dignified way of escaping the danger from Clodius. But I do not *want* to shirk it. Why? Because I prefer to fight. However, nothing is settled. Once again, if only you were here! Still, if need arise, I will send for you. Anything else? Anything? Just this, perhaps: I am convinced that everything is lost. Why be mealy-mouthed so long?

However, I'm writing this in haste and, God knows, in trepidation. In future I will tell you everything openly if I have a really trustworthy messenger available; if I write ambiguously, you will understand. In the latter case I will call myself Laelius and you Furius,[2] and convey the rest in riddles.

P.S. I am cultivating your uncle Caecilius here, and treating him with great respect. I hear you have been sent a copy of Bibulus' edicts. They are a source of bitter resentment to Pompey.

(*Ad Att.*, II, 19, 2–5)

*Caesar, having failed either to enlist or to sidetrack Cicero, who had even let out in public some criticisms of the state of affairs, now unleashed Clodius, who had become an adoptive plebeian and so eligible for the tribunate. Early in 58 Clodius proposed 'that anyone who had put Roman citizens to death uncondemned should be outlawed'. Caesar, while ostensibly deprecating retrospective action, affirmed that the execution of the Catilinarians had been illegal, and Pompey refused to disagree with him. Thereupon Cicero, despite displays of sympathy from many quarters, withdrew from Rome; and a few days later he was banished by name to*

1. As one of Caesar's twenty land commissioners.
2. Later Cicero decided that Atticus could be Atticus, but he would refrain from using his own handwriting or seal.

*beyond a radius of 500 miles from Italy. Clodius pulled down his house on the Palatine and consecrated the site to Liberty. His country houses at Tusculum and Formia were also looted and badly damaged.*

*A more dangerous opponent of the Triumvirs, the Senatorial leader Cato, was on Clodius' motion sent off to take over a new province of Cyprus, so that he was out of the way for more than two years.*

*To Atticus, at Rome*                              *Brindisi, April 29, 58 B.C.*
    I arrived at Brindisi on April 17. On the same day your men brought a letter from you, and another came two days later. I am most grateful for your kind and characteristic thoughtfulness in pressing me to stay at your house at Butrinto. It would have been a plan I should have welcomed most gladly if it were possible for me to stay there all the time:[1] I hate a crowd, I do not want to see people, I can hardly bear to look on the daylight; so the solitude there, especially in such friendly surroundings, would not have been distasteful. But as a stopping-place *en route* it is out of the way; also it is only four days from Autronius and the rest,[2] and finally you would not be there. Had I been going to settle there, a fortified place would have been an advantage, but it would be unnecessary if I were only on passage. (If I dared, I should make for Athens; indeed things *were* turning out so as to make me want to.) But now my enemies are in the neighbourhood and you are not with me, and I am afraid that that town also may be ruled to be not far enough from Italy. Nor have you let me know when I may expect you. . . .                              (*Ad Att.*, III, 7, 1)

*To Terentia, Tullia and young Marcus*            *Brindisi, April 29, 58 B.C.*
    Yes, I know I write to you less than I might; it is because not only is my whole existence wretched, but whenever I either write to you or hear from you, I break down completely and cannot bear it. If only I had not clung so much to life! Then at any rate I should have had nothing, or very little, to regret in my lifetime. True, if Fortune has preserved me for any hope of ever recovering any of my prosperity, my error was not so great; but if this misery is to be permanent, my one desire is to see you, my love, as soon as I can and to die in your arms, since neither the Gods, whom you have worshipped so devoutly,

    1. i.e. if it were beyond the 500-mile limit to which he was banished.
    2. Catilinarians in exile.

nor men, whom I have always served, have shown us any gratitude.

I have been staying at Brindisi for a fortnight with Marcus Laenius Flaccus, a very good man, who has thought more of my safety than of the risk to his own life and property, and not been deterred by the penalties of a most iniquitous decree from extending to me the due offices of friendship and hospitality. I only hope I may some day be able to show my gratitude to him: I shall certainly always feel it.

I am leaving Brindisi on April 29 and am going to Cyzicus via Macedonia. O the hopelessness, the misery of it! What am I to do? Should I ask you to come—a woman in ill-health and physically and mentally exhausted? Should I not ask you, then—and so be separated from you? I think it comes to this: if there is any hope of my return, stay and help to promote it; but if, as I fear, all is over, then find your way to me as best you can. Remember this only, that if I have you, I shall not feel I am utterly lost. But what will become of my little Tullia? You two must now see to that: I can think of no plan. But at any rate, whatever our circumstances, we must do everything for the poor girl's married happiness and reputation.[1] And then my Marcus, what will he do? How I long to have him always on my knees and in my arms! I cannot write any more now for grief. How you have fared I do not know, whether you still have anything left or, as I fear, have been completely stripped.

I hope Piso will always stick to us, as you say. As to the freeing of the household slaves, there is no need for you to be uneasy. In the first place your own were only promised that you would treat each as he deserved. Now Orpheus has behaved very well so far: apart from him, no one particularly. About the rest the arrangement was as follows: if my property was sold up, they were to have the position of freedmen of mine, if they could secure it at law; but if it continued to be mine, they were to remain my slaves, except for a very few. But these are trifles.

You encourage me to be brave and to keep on hoping that my fortunes will mend; but I wish I had any good ground for hoping so. As it is, alas, when shall I get your letters? Who will bring them to me? I would have waited for them at Brindisi, if the sailors had allowed, but they were anxious not to miss the favourable weather conditions. So finally, my Terentia, keep up your position with as

1. Her dowry had not yet been paid to her husband, Piso.

much dignity as you can. My life, my success, is past; it was not my fault, but my merit that brought my downfall. I did no wrong, unless it was in not losing my life when I lost my dignities. But since it was better for our children that I should live on, then let me bear the rest, unbearable though it be.

Clodius Philhetaerus, a loyal soul, I have sent back because he was having trouble with his eyes. Sallustius looks like being the most devoted of them all. Pescennius is most kind to me, and I hope he will always be attentive to you. Sicca had said he would accompany me, but has left us at Brindisi. Look after yourself as well as you can, and do believe that I am more upset at your misery than my own. Goodbye, dear Terentia, best and most devoted of wives, and my darling little daughter, and Marcus, now our only hope.

(*Ad Fam.*, xiv, 4)

# II

# 57 to 51 B.C.

*Caesar had now left for his province beyond the Alps, to begin his famous series of campaigns, but he kept in close touch with events at Rome. Pompey, unable to control Clodius, was soon begging Caesar to let Cicero come back. The magistrates for the year 57, led by Lentulus Spinther, a close friend who was now consul, were also in his favour. When his recall was proposed, Clodius' gangs organised riots; but Pompey instigated another tribune, Milo, to collect rival gangs and organised demonstrations among his loyal ex-servicemen throughout Italy. Finally, after sixteen months of exile spent mostly at Salonica, Cicero was recalled.*

*To Atticus, in N.W. Greece*            *Rome, September,* 57 B.C.

   ... On August 4, the very day on which the motion for my recall was carried, I left Durazzo, and arrived at Brindisi on the 5th. There my little Tullia was waiting for me, on her own birthday, which happened also to be the anniversary of the founding of the Roman colony at Brindisi, and of the Temple of Prosperity near your house. The coincidence was remarked by the crowd and I was the object of a great popular demonstration. On August 8, while still at Brindisi, I heard from Quintus that the motion had been passed in the National Assembly with extraordinary enthusiasm of all ages and classes in a wonderful crowd from all over Italy. Then, after being fêted by the good people of Brindisi, I could not get on with my journey without deputations coming from every side to congratulate me. When I approached the capital this went so far that there was not a person, of whatever rank, known to my marshal who did not come out to meet me, save only those personal enemies who could neither conceal nor deny the fact that they were my enemies. On my arrival at the Capena Gate the steps of the temples were crowded with the humblest people. They conveyed their congratulations by thundering applause, and similar crowds and applause accompanied me all the way to the Capitol. In the Forum and on the Capitol itself there was an extraordinary concourse of people.

Next day, namely September 5, I expressed my thanks to the Senate in the House. Two days after that the price of corn was very high, and crowds rushed first to the Theatre and then to the Senate shouting at Clodius' instigation that the shortage of corn was my fault.[1] The corn supply was on the Senate's agenda for those very days, and rich and poor alike were expressing the opinion that Pompey should be called upon to take the matter in hand. He himself was more than willing, and as the crowd urged me by name to make the proposal, I did so in a careful speech. Since the ex-consuls, except Messalla and Afranius, kept away on the ground that they could not safely express their opinion, it was on my motion that a decree was passed that Pompey should be approached and asked to take up the matter, and that a bill should be proposed. When this vote was read out, the people proceeded to greet my name with applause in the silly new fashion; so with the consent of all the magistrates present except one praetor and two tribunes I delivered a speech.

Next day there was a crowded house, including all the ex-consuls. They were willing to grant Pompey anything he asked. In asking for a committee of fifteen, he named me first, and said that for all purposes I should be his *alter ego*. The consuls drew up a bill appointing him sole director for five years of corn supplies all over the world; but Messius proposed an amendment giving him complete control of the exchequer, with a fleet and army thrown in and authority overriding that of Governors in their own provinces. My bill as proposed by the consuls now appears quite moderate, Messius' amendment seeming so intolerable. Pompey says he prefers the former, his friends that he prefers the latter. The consular revolt is led by Favonius. I am keeping quiet, especially as the Pontifical College has so far given no answer

1. On the ground that the crowds come in from outside to greet him caused the shortage.

about my house. If they annul its consecration,[1] I shall have a splendid site, and the consuls will value the destroyed building according to the Senate's decree. If not, they will pull down Clodius' shrine, contract for a new one on their own account, and reckon up the total compensation due to me. That is how I stand,

> For happy though but ill, for ill not worst.

My household affairs are, as you know, in an awful mess. There are also some private matters which I won't commit to writing.[2] Quintus my brother is a most devoted, good and faithful character, and I love him as he deserves. I am looking forward to your arrival, and beg you to come soon with the intention of giving me the benefit of your advice. I feel as though I were starting life all over again. Already certain persons who defended me in my absence are beginning to be secretly angry and openly envious now I have returned. I need you very badly.                     (*Ad Att.*, IV, I, 4–8)

*To Atticus, in N.W. Greece*          *Rome, November* 23, 57 B.C.
    ... On November 3 the workmen were driven off my building site by armed gangsters. My Porch of Catulus, which was being repaired under a contract made by the consuls in accordance with a decree of the Senate and had nearly got as high as the roof, was knocked down again. My brother Quintus' house was first damaged by volleys of stones thrown from my site and then, at Clodius' orders, set on fire with firebrands before the eyes of the whole city, amid an uproar of protest, I will not say from the loyalist party, which seems to have ceased to exist, but simply from the public in general. Clodius himself ran amok, bent after this mad outburst on nothing less than the murder of his opponents, canvassing the city quarter by quarter and openly offering slaves the bait of liberation. ...

    1. As a precinct sacred to Liberty, at the time of Cicero's exile. Either Cicero would get back the site and compensation for the house destroyed by Clodius, or, if the priests decided that the consecration held good, he would get compensation for house and site together from them. (The priests did annul the consecration. Cicero received adequate compensation for this house, but inadequate for those at Tusculum and Formia.)
    2. This may be a first hint of trouble with Terentia.

On November 11, as I was going down the Sacred Way, he followed me with his people. Shouts arose, stones, clubs and swords appeared— all without the least warning. We withdrew into Tettius Damio's hall, and my companions easily prevented the gang from entering. We could have killed Clodius, but I am tired of surgery and am beginning to favour treatment.

Realising now that everyone was demanding not his trial but his summary execution, Clodius proceeded to act in such a way as to make any Catiline seem a moderate. On November 12 he tried to break into Milo's house—the one on Cermalus Hill—and burn it, openly in broad daylight bringing up men with shields and drawn swords, and others with firebrands. His own headquarters for the assault were in Publius Sulla's house. But Quintus Flaccus led out some stalwarts from Milo's family mansion and killed the most prominent members of the gang. He wanted to kill Clodius himself, but he had withdrawn (?) into the interior of Sulla's house. . . .

It is now 3.0 a.m. on the 23rd as I write. Milo has already taken possession of the election-ground on the Field of Mars. Marcellus the candidate is snoring so loud that I can hear him from next door. I have just had news that Clodius' hall is quite deserted, save for a few ragamuffins with no lantern. His people are complaining that I am at the root of the trouble. They little know the spirit, or the shrewdness, of our hero. It's wonderful, his courage. I won't go into all my new forecasts. The upshot is: I don't believe the elections will be held; I think Milo will prosecute Clodius, if he hasn't killed him first; if he meets him in a riot, I can see he will kill him with his own hands. He has no scruples, and openly says he will, undismayed by my experience: *he* is never going to follow the advice of a jealous or a treacherous friend, or trust a spineless aristocracy.[1] . . .

(*Ad Att.*, IV, 3, 2–3; 5)

*Clodius continued to operate through his gangs, but these were now countered by Milo's gangs. Milo intended to have him prosecuted for breach of the peace, but Clodius evaded this by getting himself elected aedile, which secured him immunity. He at once prosecuted Milo on the same charge.*

1. As Cicero had followed the advice of the jealous Hortensius and the faithless Pompey, and trusted nobles like Lucullus—hence his exile.

*To Quintus Cicero, in Sardinia*                    *Rome, February* 15, 56 B.C.

... On February 7 Milo appeared for trial. Pompey spoke for him—or rather tried; for when he rose, Clodius' gangsters made an uproar, and this happened throughout his speech, which was interrupted not only by catcalls, but by insults and abuse. When he had concluded his speech—for I *must* admit he showed plenty of spirit in these circumstances, refused to be intimidated, and said his say, sometimes even amid silence when his authority had asserted itself—when, as I said, he had concluded, then, up got Clodius. He was greeted with such an uproar from our side, determined to return the compliment, that he lost all control of his thoughts and voice and expression. That went on from eleven, when Pompey finished, until quite one o'clock; every kind of abuse was uttered, culminating in highly obscene lampoons against Clodius and Clodia. He, white with fury, asked his partisans above the din, 'Who is starving the poor?' 'Pompey!' replied the gang. 'Who would like to go to Alexandria?'[1] 'Pompey!' 'Who do you want to go?' 'Crassus!' (He was there at the time, and not at all friendly to Milo.) At about two o'clock, apparently at a given signal, the Clodians began to spit on our men. Resentment flared up. When they began to push and try to dislodge us, our men went for them, and the gangsters fled. Clodius was thrown off the platform, and at this point I made myself scarce, for fear of anything happening to me in the riot.

The Senate was then summoned to the House. Pompey went home. But I kept away from the Senate, to avoid the dilemma of either sitting silent in such a crisis or defending Pompey and so offending the constitutionalists (he was being attacked by Bibulous, Curio, Favonius and young Servilius). The inquiry was postponed till next day. Clodius gave notice of the adjournment of the trial till February 17. On February 8 the Senate met in the Temple of Apollo, to enable Pompey to attend.[2] He made an impressive speech. That day no conclusion was reached. On the 9th, in the Temple of Apollo, the Senate voted that 'the activities prior to February 8 were seditious'. On that day Cato made a violent attack on Pompey and in a set speech arraigned him as though he were in the dock. He referred to me often, to my

1. To replace Ptolemy the Piper on the throne of Egypt, a most lucrative commission.

2. The temple was outside the walls. Pompey could get there from his house without the danger of entering the city in its present mood.

discomfiture, in the most complimentary terms, reproaching Pompey for his treachery to me. Pompey's ill-wishers let him be heard in profound silence. Pompey answered him confidently and alluded to Crassus, openly saying that he would take greater precautions to protect his own life than did Scipio Africanus, who had been murdered by Gaius Carbo.

So it seems to me that big events are now brewing. For Pompey has gathered, and confided to me, that there is a plot against his life, that Cato is backed by Crassus, while money is being supplied to Clodius; that each is being supported not only by Crassus but also by Curio, Bibulus and the rest of his critics; and that he must take energetic steps to avoid being struck down, with the commons in the Assembly generally unsympathetic, the aristocracy hostile, the Senate biased, and the younger generation out for mischief. So he is making his preparations, and has sent for men from the country districts. Clodius too is reinforcing his gang. A storm detachment is being got ready for the 17th. We shall be far the stronger side there with Milo's own forces; but a further large contingent is expected from Central and Northern Italy, to enable us also to resist Cato's proposal for an inquiry about Milo and Lentulus. . . .                    (*Ad Q.F.*, II, 3, 2–4)

*To Atticus, on his way to Rome*                    *Anzio, April*, 56 B.C.
It will be splendid of you, if you come here to stay. You will be surprised to find how well Tyrannio has arranged my books, the remains of which are much better than I thought. I would also be glad if you would send me a couple of your library boys for Tyrannio to use for glueing leaves together and other odd jobs, and tell them to get some parchment for making title-slips—'sittybae' I think you Greeks[1] call them; but only if it is convenient to you. In any case be sure and come yourself, if you can stick such a place, and bring Pilia[2] with you (which is only fair, besides being Tullia's wish).

My word, you have bought a fine troop! I hear your gladiators are fighting admirably. If you had been prepared to hire them out, you would have cleared your expenses on those two shows you gave. But more about that later. Be sure and come, and do please take steps about the library assistants.                    (*Ad Att.*, IV, 4A)

1. Teasing Atticus as being grecized.
2. Atticus' newly married wife.

*In April 56 Cicero made a blunder. His ideal was still that the Senate should rule under Pompey's guidance, instead of the Triumvirate, but he overplayed his hand. He wanted to detach Pompey, who had quarrelled with Crassus, from Caesar as well; but the method he chose, an attack on Caesar's Land Bill, only offended Pompey, whose ex-servicemen had profited by it. Caesar at once summoned Pompey, Crassus and 120 Senators who supported them to a conference at Lucca. There the Triumvirate was patched up. Caesar's command in Gaul was to be renewed for another five years; Pompey and Crassus were to be consuls in 55, the former to keep an eye on Rome and Spain, the latter to seek military glory in the East by an invasion of the kingdom of Parthia beyond the Euphrates.*

*Cicero felt that the Senatorial leaders had let him down. At a hint from Pompey he dropped his proposal, and sealed his recantation by eulogizing Caesar's victories. For the next five years he was at their beck and call, but this had one compensation: political inactivity gave him leisure for writing, and he produced his dialogues* The Orator *and* The Republic *and began* The Laws.

*Quintus Cicero was sent by his brother to join Caesar in Gaul, and went to Britain with him on his second expedition, in 54.*

*To Atticus, at Rome*                                          *Anzio, May, 56 B.C.*

What's this? Do you really imagine that I prefer my things to be read and criticised by anyone but you? Then why did I send them to someone else first? The man I sent them to was very insistent, and I had no copy. Nothing else? Well, yes (I must swallow the pill and not keep mouthing it): I felt my 'palinode' was just a shade discreditable. But goodbye to good, honest, straightforward policy. It is incredible the disloyalty of those 'leaders'[1]—leaders as they want to be and would be if they had a spark of loyalty. I felt it, I knew it: had they not led me on, then ratted and thrown me over? Even so I had resolved to collaborate with them in politics. But they have proved the same as ever, and at long last, under your guidance, I have come to my senses. You will say that you warned and advised me with a view to silence only, not to writing as well. But the truth is, I wanted to commit myself bindingly to this new connection, and leave myself no loophole for slipping back to those people, who even now, when they ought to

1. The Senatorial nobles, whom he was now abandoning for the Triumvirs. It is uncertain what writing he calls his 'palinode' or recantation.

pity me, do not cease to envy. However, I was moderate in my apotheosis—still I did write it. I will be more fulsome, if he[1] takes it kindly, and if it provokes wry faces in men who are indignant that I should possess a house that once belonged to Catulus, oblivious of the fact that I bought it from Vettius, and who say that I ought not to have rebuilt my house, but to have sold the site. (Though how's that relevant?) But they were delighted that the very speeches I was making in support of their policy were alienating me from Pompey. I must finish with them. Since those who have no power are unwilling to befriend me, let me endeavour to make friends with those who have power. You will say, 'I should have liked you to do that long ago.' I know you wanted it, and that I have been a perfect ass. But now the time has come for me to befriend myself, since there is no prospect of friendship from them on any terms.

Thank you very much for going to look after my house so often. Crassipes is eating up all my travelling-money.[2] You say, 'come straight from the journey to my villa in the suburbs'. I think it would be more convenient to come to your town house; next day, of course. Would it make any difference to you? We'll see, however. Your men have made a picture of my library with their binding and their title-slips. Please congratulate them.                    (*Ad Att.*, IV, 5)

*To Lucius Lucceius*                                    *Anzio, May, 56* B.C.

I have something to say to you which I have often tried to say face to face, only to be deterred by a kind of countrified shyness. Now we are not together I can broach the matter more boldly, since a letter does not blush. I am consumed with an extraordinary and not, I think, discreditable desire that my name should be made illustrious and renowned by a work from your pen. And though you have often assured me that such is your intention, still I trust you will forgive my impatience. The quality of your work always led me to conceive the highest expectations, but it has now surpassed them. I am so impressed, and indeed fired by it, that I wanted my doings to have the benefit of being recorded by you without a moment's delay. For I am inspired not only by the hope of achieving such immortality as posthumous

1. Caesar, or possibly Pompey.
2. By the expenses of his engagement to Tullia. (Her first husband, Piso, had died.)

fame can give, but also by a desire to relish in my lifetime the authority of your historical judgement, the token of your esteem, and the charm of your genius.

In asking this I am not unaware of the heavy burden of the works you have undertaken and already begun, but seeing that you had now almost completed your History of the Italian and Civil Wars, and had told me that you were already embarking on the subsequent period, I thought it only fair to myself to suggest that you should consider whether you preferred to weave my exploits into the general texture or (as many Greeks have done, e.g. Callisthenes in his Phocian War, Timaeus in his War of Pyrrhus, Polybius in his Numantine War, all of whom detached the wars I have mentioned from their continuous narrative) to separate the Catilinarian Conspiracy from the wars against foreign enemies. As far as my own credit goes, I do not see that it makes much difference, but it does somewhat concern my impatience that you should not wait till you get to the place, but should immediately tackle that episode and period as a whole. At the same time, if your mind is concentrated on one subject and one personality, I can imagine already how much richer and more artistic the whole thing will be.

I am well aware, of course, how presumptuous I am in first imposing such a burden on you (which you may well refuse on account of pressure of work) and then asking you besides to celebrate my own exploits. What if they should seem to you not so worthy of celebration? However, once one has overstepped the bounds of modesty one ought to be well and truly shameless. So I will blatantly ask you again and again to celebrate them with even more enthusiasm than you perhaps feel, and in this case to disregard the principles of history; and as for that Favour about whom you wrote so charmingly in one of your prefaces, declaring that you could no more be swayed by her than Xenophon's Hercules by Pleasure—if she seeks rather vehemently to prejudice you in my favour, do not spurn her, but indulge your affection for me a trifle more even than strict truth would allow.

If I can induce you to undertake this, the subject will, I am convinced, be worthy of your talent and eloquence. I think a fair-sized volume could be made out of events from the beginning of the conspiracy down to my return. In it you will be able to use your expert understanding of political unrest, both in explaining the causes of revolution and in suggesting remedies for its evils, criticising what you think deserves condemnation and giving a reasoned commendation of what you approve; and if you think fit, as your custom is, to be exceptionally outspoken, you will stigmatise the disloyalty, deceit and treachery that many have displayed towards me. Moreover my fortunes will supply you with plenty of variety, a copious source of pleasure which, given your literary skill, could rivet the reader's attention. For there is nothing better suited to please a reader than the changes and chances of Fortune; and however unwelcome these were for me to experience, they will none the less make good reading. For the recollection in tranquillity of troubles past is not without its charm. The rest of the world indeed, which has not experienced any suffering of its own, and can look upon the misfortunes of others without pain, derives a certain pleasure from the emotion of pity itself. Which of us in contemplating the death of Epaminondas at Mantinea is not pleased even as he pities? He did not ask for the javelin to be pulled out of him until he had been assured that his shield was safe, so that in spite of the pain of his wound he died gloriously with his mind at rest. Whose sympathy is not aroused and sustained by the story of the exile and return of Themistocles?[1] The fact is, that a mere chronicle of events does not interest us much, any more than the entries in the official almanac. But the uncertain and varied fortunes of a man who often rises to prominence provoke admiration, suspense, joy, sorrow, hope and fear; and if they end in a striking *dénouement*, the mind enjoys one of the greatest pleasures that reading can give. . . .

*(Ad Fam.*, v, 12, 1–5)

*To Atticus, at Rome*                                  *In the country, May,* 56 B.C.

I was as sorry as I should be to hear about Lentulus Niger: we have lost a sound man and a great personality, one in whom extreme strength of character was tempered by a fund of kindness. We have some consolation, poor though it be, in the fact that we cannot grieve for his own sake—not for the general reasons given by Saufeius and your Epicureans,[2] but just because he loved his country so well that

1. Either Cicero or a scribe had made a mistake here. Themistocles never returned. Epaminondas of Thebes died in 362 in the hour of victory over Sparta.
2. The Epicurean view that death, being simply annihilation, was no evil was given supreme expression by the poet Lucretius.

I can only think it a godsend that he was spared its conflagration. For what could be more degrading than our present life, especially mine? You, though you have a political bent, have no special yoke of slavery; you are only a slave like everyone else; but I, who am thought mad if I say what is right about politics, servile if I say what is expedient, crushed and helpless if I say nothing—what must I be suffering? What I do suffer, believe me, and it is all the more bitter because I cannot complain without seeming ungrateful to you. Could I not choose to remain inactive and retire to the haven of leisure? No chance. Then to arms and fight! What, and be a subaltern after refusing to be a commander? There's no choice. You yourself would approve, and I wish to goodness I had always taken your advice. Now it's only a matter of 'make the most of what you've got'. No, I'm damned if I can, and I sympathise with Philoxenus, who preferred to go back to prison. Still, I am spending my time here precisely in thinking out how to make the most of it, and when we meet you will strengthen my purpose. . . .

I sent a letter to Lucceius asking him to write about my doings. Be sure and get it from him—it's a very nice piece of writing—and urge him to hurry up, and thank him for replying that he would do it. Go to see my house as often as you can. And please say a word to Vestorius: he has been most generous to me.          (*Ad Att.*, IV, 6, 1–2; 4)

*To Lentulus Spinther, Governor of Cilicia     Rome, late August*, 56 B.C.
     . . . You asked about the political situation. The breach could not be wider, but the energy is all on one side. Those who are superior in wealth, arms and influence seem to me to have profited so much by the stupidity and halfheartedness of their opponents that they are now superior even in prestige. Consequently, with hardly any dissentient voices, they have been granted by the Senate everything which they previously thought they could not obtain even from the popular assembly without provoking a riot. Thus Caesar has been voted pay for his troops and ten subordinate commanders, and exemption from being superseded under the Sempronian Law[1] has been easily obtained for him.

     1. This required the Senate to specify, before Consuls were elected, the provinces they were to govern after their year of office. If the Senate had now named Gaul, it would have implied automatic supersession of Caesar in 54 B.C. They were induced not to name it.

I write somewhat briefly on this topic, because the state of affairs is not to my liking. But I do write nevertheless, to impress upon you a lesson which, with all my life-long devotion to literature, I have discovered from experience rather than from books: learn before you come to grief that one should not contemplate safety without honour, nor yet honour without safety. . . .                    (*Ad Fam.*, I, 7, 10)

*To Lentulus Spinther, Governor of Cilicia*          Rome, *January*, 55 B.C.
On all matters concerning you I advise you to find out what has been done and decided, and what Pompey has undertaken, from Marcus Plaetorius, who has played not merely a part but a leading part in these matters, and has neglected no service to you that devotion or prudence or diligence could dictate. He will likewise tell you all about the state of public affairs, which it is not easy to describe in a letter. Not but what these affairs are in the hands of our friends,[1] and so securely indeed that it seems unlikely that our generation will see any change. As for me, I do what you yourself advised me, and what loyalty and expediency demand: I am attaching myself to the fortunes of the man whom you decided to attach to yourself when my fortunes were at stake.[2] But you will realise how hard it is to give up one's political convictions, especially when they are right and justified. However, I am adapting myself to his wishes, since I cannot honourably differ from him, and I am not doing so hypocritically, as some may perhaps imagine; for I am so much influenced by my predilection, indeed affection for Pompey, that what is useful and pleasing to him has now become equivalent to true and right for me. Nor, I think, would even his opponents be wrong if, since they can be no match for him, they gave up the struggle.

I have indeed this further consolation, that I am in the position of being sure of the full approval of all, whether I defend Pompey's policy, or keep silence, or, as I would prefer above all, retire to my literary studies, which I shall certainly do if it is compatible with my friendship for Pompey. I used to look forward, after a life of high office and strenuous endeavour, to speaking with prestige in the House and preserving an independent attitude in politics; but all that is gone, for others no less than for me. It is now a choice between

1. So he now calls the Triumvirs.
2. Lentulus courted Pompey when seeking to get Cicero back from exile.

humbly agreeing with a few people, and disagreeing to no purpose.

I am writing this chiefly with the object of inducing you to take stock of your attitude as well. The whole essence of the Senate, law courts and State in general has changed. A quiet life is what we should pray for; and it looks as if the powers that be are ready to give it us, if certain persons can show more tolerance of their supremacy. The old idea of the courageous and upright senator with his consular dignity may as well be forgotten. It has been lost through the fault of those who alienated from the Senate a class that was closely bound to it and a man of great distinction.[1] . . .      (*Ad Fam.*, 1, 8, 1–4)

*To Atticus, at Rome*              *Cuma, near Naples, April* 22, 55 B.C.

Pozzuoli is full of rumours that Ptolemy has been restored to his throne. Please let me know if there is any more definite news. I am feasting here on Faustus' library, in case you thought the local produce[2] of Pozzuoli and the Lucrine Lake was the attraction. I don't lack that either, but the truth is that the more I am robbed of my relish for material pleasures by the thought of the political situation, the more comfort and recreation I find in literature, and I would rather be sitting in the little chair you keep under your bust of Aristotle than in the presidential chair of Pompey and Crassus, and be taking a walk at home with you than here with the man I see I shall have to walk with.[3] Where that walk will lead me fate or whatever god may be will decide.

My own garden walk and baths and their surroundings I should be glad if you would inspect when you can, and urge Philotimus to get on, so that I may have something to compare with you in that sphere.

Pompey arrived at his house at Cuma yesterday the 21st, and immediately sent a man to pay his respects. I am going to call on him this morning.                                        (*Ad Att.*, IV, 10)

*To Marcus Marius, near Naples*              *Rome, September,* 55 B.C.

If it was some pain or the poorness of your health that kept you from coming to the festival, that was to the credit of your luck rather than your judgement; but if it was that you thought nothing of these

1. The Knights and Pompey.
2. Oysters.
3. Pompey.

things which the rest admire so much, and were unwilling to come
although your health would have allowed it, then I am doubly pleased,
both at your freedom from bodily weakness and at your strength of
mind in turning down what others wrongly admire—always provided
that you made good use of your leisure, as indeed you had a wonderful
chance of doing, left almost to yourself in those lovely surroundings.
But of course you did. I can see you all those days spending the
morning dipping into a book in your bedroom there, with its window
that you made specially to open up the view over the Bay of Stabia,
while those who had left you behind were looking half-asleep at
comedians on the public stage; and spending the rest of the day on
pleasures arranged of your own free choice, while we had to sit
through things officially sanctioned by Spurius Maecius.[1]

If you want to know, the festival was altogether on a most elaborate
scale, but not to your taste, if I may judge by my own. To begin with,
actors returned to the stage out of respect for the occasion who, I
thought, had left it out of respect for themselves. Your old favourite,
our friend Aesopus, was in such a state that everyone present was glad
to let him retire. When he began to take the actors' oath, his voice
failed him at the crucial point: 'If I wittingly pervert. . . .' Need I tell
you more? You know what else happens at festivals. This did not even
have the charm that less pretentious ones have, since all the fun was
lost in the elaboration of the spectacle, with which you, I know, would
have been only too willing to dispense. For what pleasure can there
be in six hundred mules in the *Clytemnestra* or three thousand wine-
bowls in the *Trojan Horse*, or variegated cavalry and infantry equipment in some battle-scene or other? These excited the admiration of
the groundlings, but would have added nothing to your enjoyment.
Whereas if you meanwhile were paying attention to your Protogenes
(provided he read you anything rather than my speeches), why, you
were enjoying yourself considerably more than any of us. For I don't
expect you would have regretted missing the Greek and Oscan farces,
especially as you can see Oscan farces any time you like, in your local
council, and you are so anti-Greek that you even refuse to go home by
Greek Street. And why should I think you would hanker after the
athletes, you who scorned the gladiators? Pompey himself confesses
he wasted his time and money on them. There remain the animal-

1. The licenser of plays.

hunts, twice daily for five days—very lavish, no one denies. But what pleasure can it be to a man of refinement when either a powerless man is torn by a very powerful beast, or else a magnificent beast is spitted on a hunting-spear? In any case, if such things are worth seeing, you have seen them often; and we who were there saw nothing new. The last day was devoted to the elephants. The sight caused great astonishment among the common herd, but there was no pleasure in it; indeed there was a reaction almost to pity, and a kind of feeling that this animal had something in common with the human race.

During these days of the stage productions, in case you should think that I was not only happy but also quite free, I was sweating blood over the case of your acquaintance Caninius Gallus. If only I had as indulgent a public as Aesopus, I swear I should gladly retire from my profession and live with you and people of our sort. I was tired of it even before, when I still had the stimulus of youth and ambition, and what's more, I was allowed not to defend people I did not choose; but now, as things are, life simply isn't worth living, since I can look for no reward for my labours, and I am compelled sometimes to defend men who have not done very well by me at the request of those who have. So I am looking for any excuse for living at last as my own master, and I strongly commend and approve of you and your principle of leisure; and I put up more willingly with our seeing each other less often when I reflect that, if you were at Rome, I could not enjoy the pleasure of your society, nor you any pleasure there may be in mine, because of my extremely tiresome affairs. If ever I can relax —relaxation, not release, is all I ask—I will even teach you yourself, who have thought about nothing else for years, how a civilised life should be led. You meanwhile must take care of your health, as you do, and keep fit, so that you will be able to make the round of my houses and gad about with me in a litter.

This has been a longer letter than usual, out of the abundance, not of my leisure, but of my affection for you, because you hinted in one of your letters, if you remember, that I should write you something to reconcile you to not having gone to the festival. If I have achieved that object, I am glad; if not, at least I can console myself with the thought that in future you will come to the festivals and pay me a visit, and not have to rely on a letter from me for such enjoyment as you may hope to derive from them.                    (*Ad Fam.*, VII, I)

*To Julius Caesar, in Gaul*                    *Rome, Spring,* 54 B.C.

You will see from this letter how convinced I am that you are a second self to me, not only in my own concerns but in those of my friends. I had intended to take Gaius Trebatius with me wherever I went abroad, so as to bring him home enriched with every benefit that my care and attention could bestow. But now that Pompey has delayed starting for longer than I expected, and also that a certain hesitation, for reasons not unknown to you, seems likely to prevent, or at least hold up, my own departure, here is what I have taken upon myself: I am beginning to hope that Trebatius may look to you for what he expected from me, and I must confess I promised him your goodwill as profusely as formerly I promised him my own. Then a remarkable incident occurred which seemed a confirmation of my opinion or a guarantee of your kindness. I was having quite a serious talk with Balbus at my house about this very Trebatius when I was handed a letter from you with the postscript, 'About Marcus (?) Orfius whom you recommend to me, I'm quite prepared to make him King of Gaul; but you can put him down to Lepta's account, if you like, and send someone else for me to promote.' Balbus and I both threw up our hands in amazement. It was such a happy coincidence that it seemed a case of providence rather than chance.

So I am sending Trebatius to you as chosen originally on my own initiative but now also in response to your invitation. And I trust, my dear Caesar, that you will welcome him with all your usual kindness, and concentrate on him all the goodwill I could induce you to display to friends of mine. As to his character, I assure you, not with that cliché of mine about which you rightly teased me when I used it in my letter concerning Milo, but in the honest Roman language of sensible men, that there is no straighter character, no better or more intelligent man than he. I should add that he is at the top of his profession of civil law, with an extraordinary memory and vast learning.[1] I will not ask for him the rank of colonel or prefect or any specific favour, leaving everything to your kindness and generosity; but neither will I raise any objection if you see fit to confer upon him these little marks of distinction. I commit him entirely, in legal phrase, 'from my hand into your hand'—a hand as noted for good faith as it is for martial deeds.

1. C. Trebatius Testa became one of the famous jurists of Rome, and a friend of Horace.

Excuse my being a bit of a bore over this: I know you don't suffer it gladly, but I fancy you will in this case.

My best wishes for your good health. Please continue to think kindly of me.                                      (*Ad Fam.*, VII, 5)

*To Quintus Cicero, in Gaul*                    *Rome, June 3, 54 B.C.*

On June 2, when I arrived at Rome, I got your letter dated from Piacenza, and on the next day another, dated from nine miles beyond Lodi, along with one from Caesar full of goodwill, solicitude and pleasantness of every kind. These symptoms are important, indeed of the greatest importance: they bear directly on our prestige and high standing. But you must believe, knowing me, that what I value most in all this I have already, first of all your own devotion to the cause of our common status, and secondly Caesar's being so attached to me, which I rate higher than all the honours he would have me expect at his hands.

I was extremely pleased with the letter he sent with yours which began by saying how delighted he was at your arrival and the memories it brought of our old intimacy, and went on to tell me that, although I was bound to be sad and miss you while you were away, I should be glad that you were with him in particular. So while it was a brotherly act on your part to urge me to focus all my enthusiasm on him, I can assure you I am already hastening to do so. Yes indeed, I am burning with enthusiasm for him; and as it often happens that a traveller in a hurry, having got up later than he intended, through putting on extra speed reaches his destination sooner than if he had been up before daybreak, so I, who in the matter of cultivating his friendship overslept so long (despite your continual efforts to wake me!) will make up for my slowness with horses and (since you say he liked my poem) with the chariot of poetry. Just you give me Britain to paint with my brush and colours supplied by you!

But what am I doing? What time can I hope to have free, especially if I stay at Rome, as he asks me to do? Still, I'll see. Perhaps, as usual, love will find a way. He even thanked me in most witty and polite terms for sending Trebatius to him, observing that he had previously had no one on his whole staff who knew how to draw up a recognisance! I addressed to him my request for the rank of colonel for Marcus Curtius—if I had addressed it to Domitius the consul, he would have thought he was being laughed at, since no day passes without his complaining that he can't even make anyone a colonel, and even in the Senate he twitted his colleague Appius with having gone to meet Caesar at Lucca specially to get someone made colonel. But my request was for next year, that being Curtius' wish.

In the matters of our political attitude and feuds, whatever you advise, I assure you I am and shall be as wax in your hands. The state of Rome is as follows: there is some hope of elections being held, but no certainty; there is some idea of a dictatorship, but even that is uncertain; calm reigns in the Forum, but it is the calm of a decrepit rather than a contented state. As for my speeches in the Senate, they are such that others agree with them more than I do myself:

These are the fruits of miserable strife

(*Ad Q.F.*, II, 14/13)

*To Quintus Cicero, in Britain*          *Arpino, September 28, 54 B.C.*

I have been recovering from the intense heat—the worst I can remember—at Arpino, and enjoying the loveliness of the river, having left my protégés in charge of Philotimus for the annual festival.[1] I was at your place at Arce on the 10th. There I found Mescidius with Philoxenus[2] and saw the water for which they were making a conduit not far from the house flowing quite nicely, especially considering the drought. They said they were going to collect it in considerably larger quantities. All was well with Herus.

At your Manilian place I found Diphilus going slow even for Diphilus. Still, he had finished everything except the baths, the cloister and the aviary. I liked the house enormously for the dignity of its paved colonnade, which I only realised when I saw the whole length open and the columns polished. It will all depend on the stucco harmonising, and I will see to that. The pavement seemed to be getting well laid. I did not care for some of the ceilings, and ordered them to be changed. They showed me the place in the colonnade where you had written you wanted a porch made, but I liked it better as it is. I didn't think there was room for a porch, and it is not usual to find one except in houses where there is a larger hall, nor would it be big enough

1. Important people often provided members of their 'tribe' with seats for the games. Philotimus was one of Terentia's freedmen.
2. Contractors. Herus was a bailiff, Diphilus an architect.

to have bedrooms and suchlike apartments opening off it. As it is, it will make either a decent vaulted chamber or an admirable summer room. If you still don't agree, please write at once.

In the baths I have moved the hot chamber to the other corner of the dressing-room, because it was so placed that the chimney would be under the bedrooms. The fair-sized bedroom and the other winter room I liked enormously, since they were both spacious and in the right position, on one side of the cloister, that next to the baths. Diphilus had got the columns neither perpendicular nor opposite each other. He'll have to take them down, of course. Perhaps some day he'll learn how to use a plumb-line and measuring-tape. All things considered, I expect Diphilus' work will be finished in a few months' time: Caesius, who went round with me, keeps a watchful eye on him. . . .

I was at Laterium on the 13th. I inspected the private road and found it so good that it was more like a public highway, except for a stretch of 150 yards I paced out from the little bridge by the temple of Furina in the direction of Satricum. This had been surfaced with earth instead of gravel—it will have to be altered—and this part of the road is pretty steep. I realised it could not have gone any other way, especially as you did not want it to go through either Locusta's or Varro's land. Varro had made up the part opposite his farm properly, but Locusta had not touched his bit. I'll get on to him at Rome and hope to stir him up, and will also make inquiries of Marcus Taurus, who is now in town, about leading water through his farm. I hear he gave you a promise. . . .

I am all in favour of your carrying out the proposed additions; though as it stands the house is like a demure moralist reproving the frivolity of her neighbours. At any rate, you'll enjoy having the extension. I congratulated the gardener: he has made the ivy so mantle everything, both the foundation wall and the spaces in the colonnade, that now those Greek statues look as if they were topiary artists pointing it out for our approval. Again, the bathing-place is as cool and mossy as can be. . . .               (*Ad Q.F.*, III, 1, 1–2; 4–5)

*To Quintus Cicero*               *Tusculum, near Rome, October*, 54 B.C.

You asked me about the dialogue I began to write when I was at Cuma.[1] Well, I have not been idle, nor am I now, but I have often

1. *The Republic.*

changed the whole idea and arrangement of the work. I had already completed two books of it, in which I represented a conversation as taking place during the Nine Days Holiday in the consulship of Tuditanus and Aquilius[1] between Scipio Africanus (shortly before his death) and Laelius, Philus, Manilius, Publius Rutilius, Quintus Tubero and Laelius' sons-in-law, Fannius and Scaevola. The conversation was to be spread over nine days and nine books, dealing with the best form of State and the best kind of citizen. I must say, the work was excellently constructed and the eminence of the interlocutors lent weight to their utterances. But when those books were being read over to me at my house at Tusculum in the presence of Sallust, he suggested that the treatment could be given much more authority if I made myself the speaker on the Republic, especially as I was no mere academic writer like Heraclides Ponticus, but an ex-consul who had played a leading part in the highest affairs of State; that speeches attributed to men so long dead would have an air of unreality; that in my work on the principles of rhetoric I had chosen happily, in that, while keeping myself out of the speakers, I had attributed the speeches nevertheless to men whom I had seen in the flesh; and finally, that Aristotle had spoken in his own person in his works *On the Republic* and *On Individual Eminence*.

He shook my purpose, the more so as I had been debarring myself from reference to the most important upheavals in our State, since they took place after the lifetime of my interlocutors. Previously that had been precisely my object—to avoid offending anyone if I ran on into our own times. As it is, I shall both beware of that and yet make myself the speaker along with you. Still, when I come to Rome I will send you the original books, since you will no doubt conceive that I did not recast them without some heart-burning. . . .

You say you polished off four tragedies in sixteen days: can you have been borrowing from someone? And are you looking for emotion, after writing your *Electra* and *Trojan Women*? Don't be lazy, and don't think the Greek proverb 'Know Thyself' means only to curb our arrogance, but also that we should realise our good qualities. But please send them to me, and the *Erigone* too.

(*Ad Q.F.*, III, 5, 1–2; 7)

1. 129 B.C.

*To Trebatius Testa, in Gaul*        *Rome, December,* 54 B.C.

I have read your letter and gathered from it that our Caesar thinks you a most learned counsel. You can congratulate yourself on being where you are, in a region where you pass for a man of learning. But if only you had gone over to Britain, you would certainly have found yourself the greatest expert in all that great island! However (you must forgive my teasing you, since you asked for it), I am just a shade jealous of you for being actually sent for by one whom others, not because he is too proud but because he is too busy, cannot hope to approach.

But your letter told me nothing about your own affairs, which I swear are just as important to me as my own. I'm terribly afraid you may be cold in your winter quarters; so I advise you to use a really good stove; Lord Justices Mucius and Manilius concur, especially as your kit is rather scanty. Not but what I hear you're having quite a warm time up there,[1] news which made me damned anxious on your account. But you are much more cautious as a warrior than as a barrister, since for all your passion for swimming you declined to swim in the Channel, or to inspect the British charioteers, though at Rome you wouldn't let us cheat you out of the meanest gladiator-match.

But joking apart, you know how conscientiously I have written to Caesar about you, but I know also how often. Indeed I had given it up for the time being, for fear of seeming to doubt the goodwill of a man who has been most generous and a true friend to me. However, in my last letter I thought I should jog his memory, and did so; please let me know what success I had, and at the same time all about your position and plans. I am longing to know how you are getting on, what you expect to happen, and how long you think we shall be deprived of you. For you must take it from me that the one consolation which reconciles me to your absence is the thought that it is to your own advantage; if this is not the case, we are both utter fools, I for not dragging you back to Rome, you for not flying back. One meeting of ours, whether for business or fun, will surely be worth more than all our enemies put together, or even than 'our brothers-in-arms' the Haedui.[2] So tell me about everything as soon as you can:

> Comfort or counsel you shall have, or cash.

> *(Ad Fam.,* VII, 10)

1. Owing to a rising of the Gauls.
2. A Gallic people so designated by the Senate.

# III

# May 51 to December 50 B.C.

*In 54 Julia, who had been as devoted a wife to Pompey as she was daughter to Caesar, died. Next year Crassus was killed at Carrhae, where the Parthians utterly defeated his army. The Triumvirate was thus shattered, and when in 52 there were continual riots (in one of which Milo killed Clodius at Bovillae), Pompey was elected sole consul. Power was thus divided more or less equally between him and the absent Caesar.*

*At this time a new law was passed that ex-consuls and ex-praetors should not proceed to govern provinces until five years after their term of office ended, instead of the next year. (This was to check bribery: candidates used to offer heavy bribes on the security of the fortune they would shortly make by exploiting their province.) One consequence was that, in the shortage of ex-consuls and ex-praetors of five years' standing, the Senate called on Cicero to be governor for 51–50 of Cilicia, the S.E. strip of Asia Minor, to which were attached Cyprus and some odd departments north of the Taurus mountains. At the same time Bibulus was appointed to govern Syria. Both provinces were thought to be threatened by the Parthians.*

*Reluctantly Cicero consented, choosing his brother as lieutenant, and Pomptinus, a good sailor, as Chief of Staff. Young Marcus and Quintus accompanied their fathers.*

*To Atticus, at Rome*          *? Minturnae, May,* 51 B.C.

I did indeed see how you felt at our parting, and I can vouch for my own feelings. So you must make doubly sure that no new decree is passed which would make our unhappy separation last for more than a year. . . .

Now I come to the marginal postscript to your letter in which you gave me a hint with regard to your sister.[1] This is how things stand. When I got home to Arpino and my brother joined me, we talked first of all about you, and at some length. From that I got on to the conversation you and I had about your sister at my place at Tusculum. I have never seen anyone so sweet or so conciliatory as my brother was on this occasion to your sister; if there was any ill-feeling on the score of expense, it was not apparent. So much for that day.

Next day we left Arpino. In view of the date, Quintus stayed at his place at Arce; I was due at Aquino, but we dined at Arce. You know the farm. When we arrived Quintus said very nicely, 'Pomponia, you ask the women, and meanwhile I'll look after the boys.' To my mind nothing could have been pleasanter—not only his words, but his intention and expression. Yet she said in our hearing, 'I, the mistress, seem to be only a stranger here.' I think the real trouble was that Statius had been sent ahead to get dinner for us. Quintus turned to me and said, 'You see what I have to put up with, day in, day out.' 'Is that all?' you may ask. It was a great deal; and I was quite roused myself. Her words and expression were so rude and uncalled-for. I concealed my distress. We all took our places for dinner except her; even so, Quintus sent her out something, but she refused it. In short, I never saw anything so polite as my brother or so rude as your sister; and I've left out a lot of things that upset me more at the time than they did Quintus himself.

Then I went on to Aquino. Quintus stayed at Arce and joined me next day at Aquino, where he told me that she had refused to sleep with him, and on parting had behaved as I had seen her do. Well? You can tell her this from me: in my opinion she was not at all nice that day.

I have gone on longer perhaps than was necessary to show you that in the matter of giving good advice you too have a part to play. For the rest, please finish off all my commissions before you leave, write to me about everything, get Pomptinus moving, let me know when you have started, and don't forget that there is nothing in the world so dear and precious to me as yourself.

1. Pomponia, Quintus Cicero's wife.

I parted most affectionately at Minturnae with Aulus Torquatus, an excellent fellow; kindly let him know when you see him that I have mentioned him to you.                                       (*Ad Att.*, v, 1; 3–5)

*To keep him informed during his absence, since Atticus might be away in N.W. Greece, Cicero enlisted Caelius, a brilliant, amusing, unprincipled young protégé of his. Caelius had supplanted his friend the poet Catullus as lover of Clodia, and when he dropped her, had been rescued from her claws by Cicero.*

*To Cicero, from Marcus Caelius*                    *Rome, late in May,* 51 B.C.

With regard to the promise I gave you when we parted, that I would write most diligently about everything that happens in the capital, I have been at pains to secure the services of a man who would go minutely into every detail—so minutely that I'm afraid you may find his efforts too long-winded. However, I know how meticulous you are, and how everyone abroad loves to be told about the slightest thing that happens at home. But I must beg you not to think that in delegating this job to someone else I have been off-hand in fulfilling my undertaking. It is not that I should not enjoy every minute devoted to thinking of you, busy though I am and, as you know, a very bad correspondent; but I am sure you will agree that the very size of the roll I am sending herewith is ample excuse. Heaven knows how much leisure one would need even to write out all this, let alone take note of it: you will find there every single Decree of the Senate, *bon mot*, story or rumour. In case this sample is not to your liking, please let me know, to save me from spending money only to bore you. If anything special happens in public affairs which is beyond the scope of such clerks, I will myself write you a careful account of what happened, what people's reactions were, and what the result is expected to be. As things are, there is nothing much in the air. Those rumours about elections north of the Po only kept warm as far as Cuma; when I got to Rome, I did not hear so much as a whisper about them. And Marcellus, by holding up his proposal[1] about the succession to the governorship of Gaul and postponing it (as he told me himself) until

1. The proposal was that Caesar should give up his provinces on March 1, 50, on the pretext (hardly justifiable) that the war in Gaul was over.

June 1, has naturally compelled people to express the same opinion of him as they did when we were at Rome together.

If you ran into Pompey, as you were hoping, let me know what you thought about him, what he told you, and which way he seemed to be inclining (he often says one thing and thinks another, and has not the wit to be able to conceal his true aims). As for Caesar, rumours about him are frequent and not very nice, but only whisperers bring them. One says he has lost his horse—a horse? no doubt he has;[1] another, that the Seventh Legion has taken a beating, and that he himself is cut off from the rest of the army and surrounded near Beauvais. No certain news has arrived yet; nor are even these vague rumours in general circulation, only an open secret in circles known to you; Domitius repeats them with his hands to his mouth.

You died on May 24—according to reports spread by loafers outside the courts (I should like to see *them* dead); the rumour was all over the Forum and the City that you had been murdered on the road by Quintus Pompeius. As I happened to know that Quintus Pompeius was at that moment taking a slimming course[2] at Bauli and was so hungry that I was quite sorry for the man, I took it calmly, and only hoped that this canard would clear the air for us of any danger that might be hanging over you.

Your friend Plancus is at Ravenna, and in spite of a large bounty from Caesar is not prosperous or even comfortably off.

Your volumes of *The Republic* are universally popular.

(Ad Fam., VIII, 1)

*To Atticus*                                    *Athens, June 29, 51 B.C.*

I reached Athens on June 25, and have been waiting for three days now for Pomptinus without getting any definite information about his arrival. I am with you in spirit all the time, you may be sure; and though I should have been thinking of you in any case, I do so the more vividly because there are traces of you everywhere to remind me. Why, we never seem to talk of any other subject. But perhaps you would rather hear something of myself. Very well.

So far no public or private expense has been incurred either for me

1. Pun, hard to render, on *eques*, singular, as used for cavalry and for a horseman.
2. Or possibly, letting out boats.

or for any of my staff; nothing has been requistioned either under Caesar's Law or from anyone on whom we have been billeted; all my staff have taken it to heart that my reputation must not suffer. So far so good. This has been noticed, and has caused much favourable comment in Greek circles. For the rest, I am taking great care to do what I feel you would approve. But let us keep our applause till the play is finished.

All other circumstances are such as to make me often curse my incompetence in not having somehow got out of this business. Could anything be less in my line? How true the saying is

*à chacun son métier!*

'Already?' you will say, 'but you haven't even got into the business yet.' Too true, and I think the worst is to come. But I'm putting a brave face on it, and carrying it off, I think, though in my heart of hearts I'm hating it. Every day I come across so many examples of ill-tempered or ill-mannered or utterly tactless and arrogant utterances and omissions. I won't go into details, not to keep things from you, but because they are hard to put down in black and white. You will admire my 'closeness' when I get back; I get such practice in that virtue. . . .

Anything else? Nothing really, except this: I am delighted with Athens, with the city itself, that is, and its monuments, and with the people's affection for you and goodwill, if I may say so, towards me; but as for my philosophy (or yours, if you like), it's all topsy-turvy; what there is I get from Aristus, where I'm staying. I haven't let Quintus have your (or our) friend Xeno: though he's so near that we're together all day.

Please let me know as soon as you can what your ideas are, what you are doing, your changes of address, and particularly when you will be at Rome.                                          (*Ad At.*, v, 10, 1–3; 5)

*The following famous letter is especially interesting because Memmius, now in exile for bribery, is no other than the unworthy noble to whom Lucretius had dedicated his passionate poem vindicating the Epicurean philosophy.*

*To Gaius Memmius, at Mitylene*          *Athens, end of June,* 51 B.C.

Although I could not make up my mind beforehand whether I was going to be more distressed or glad at meeting you in Athens, because while the injustice you have suffered was a source of sorrow to me, the philosophic spirit in which you are bearing it was a source of joy, still I wish now that I had met you; for the pain has not, after all, been much relieved by my not seeing you, and such pleasure as is possible would definitely have been enhanced by seeing you. So I shall not hesitate to take steps to see you as soon as I can at all conveniently do so. Meanwhile there is a piece of business which can be discussed with you and, I trust, finished off by letter, and I will broach it now. But first of all I will ask you not to do anything against your will for my sake, but to grant me a request, which you will perceive to mean a lot to me and nothing to you, only if you are first satisfied that you are doing so gladly.

With Patro the Epicurean I see eye to eye, save that I differ from him violently in philosophy. Both in the early days at Rome, when he was paying his respects to you too and to all your friends, he made a point of cultivating my acquaintance, and recently, when he got satisfaction concerning his privileges and remuneration, he found in me almost his chief defender and friend. He had originally been introduced and recommended to me by Phaedrus, of whom I had the highest opinion, as a philosopher in my young days before I got to know Philo, and even subsequently as a good and charming and obliging person. Well, this Patro wrote to me while I was at Rome asking me to intercede for him and beg you to let him have that tumble-down house or whatnot that once belonged to Epicurus, but I did not in fact write to you, because I did not want your plans for building to be interfered with by any vicarious plea from me. But when I got to Athens and he asked me again to write to you to the same effect, I consented simply because all your friends assured me that you had abandoned that particular building project. If this is so, and you are sure that it now makes no difference to you, please, if your feelings have been hurt in any way by some people's unreasonableness (I know the race), take a lenient view, either out of your great kindness or even just as a compliment to me. If you ask my own opinion I cannot see why he should be so very keen, nor why you should be objecting, except that there is much less reason why you should be put to needless trouble than he.

However, I know you are well aware of Patro's plea and the case he makes. His position, his duty, the rights of testators, the prestige of Epicurus, the solemn injunction of Phaedrus, the preservation of the estate and home and relics of famous men—for all these things at stake he says he feels responsible. We may laugh at the whole tenor and system of the man's philosophy, if we are bent on finding fault with his eagerness over this; but good gracious, since we are not serious enemies of Epicurus and his devotees, perhaps we can forgive this fellow for being so much exercised about it! Even if he is at fault there's more folly than knavery in it.

But to be brief (for the truth will out), I love Pomponius Atticus as a brother; nothing in the world is so near and dear to me. And he—not that he is typical of the Epicureans, being a highly cultivated and civilised man, but because he is very fond of Patro and was devoted to Phaedrus—he, this least pushing, least importunate of men, has badgered me over this more than over anything ever before; and he is sure that I have only to say the word to obtain your consent, even if you were still going to build. As it is, if he hears that you have given up the idea of building and I have still not prevailed upon you, he will not think that you have been ungenerous to me, but that I have been indifferent to him. So I beg you to write to your people to say that that decree (or 'memorandum' as they call it here) or the Areopagus can be revoked with your full consent.

But as I said at the start, please satisfy yourself that you will do this gladly for my sake rather than just do it. Only remember, if you do what I ask, I shall be extremely grateful.        (*Ad Fam.*, XIII, I)

*To Caelius, at Rome*                              *Athens, July 6,* 51 B.C.

What's this? Do you imagine I commissioned you to tell me about the matching of gladiators, the adjournment of trials, the Chrestus robbery, and such things as no one would dare retail to me when I am at Rome? Now just see the confidence I think you worthy of—and with good reason, for I never knew a man with such a *flair* for politics: I'm not wanting you to write me a day-to-day commentary even on the most important political matters, unless there is anything that touches me personally; others will write, many will bring news, rumour itself will contribute much. What I look for from you is not the past nor the present, but a far-sighted man's forecast of the future so that when I perceive in your letters the ground-plan of the State, I may be in a position to know how the building will turn out.

However, I have no complaint to make against you so far: nothing has occurred which you had a better chance of foreseeing than any of us, and myself especially, since I spent several days with Pompey talking about nothing else but politics—things which neither could nor should be committed to writing. I will only say this, that Pompey is splendidly patriotic, and ready in heart and head for every political precaution that may prove necessary.

> Give him thyself: with open arms,
> be sure, he'll welcome thee.

For as to who is a patriot and who is not, he agrees entirely with our general opinion. . . .                    (*Ad Fam.*, II, 8, 1–2)

*To Atticus, at Rome*                    *Isle of Delos, July* 12, 51 B.C.
Sailing is quite a business, even in July. It has taken us six days to get from Athens to Delos. We left the Piraeus on the 6th and got to Cape Lombarda with a troublesome wind which kept us there over the 7th. On the 8th we had a pleasant crossing to Ceos; from there to Gyaros, with the wind fierce but not against us; thence we made Syros, and from there came on to Delos, in both cases with uncomfortable speed. You know these open Rhodian boats from experience; there's no worse craft in a swell. So I'm inclined to take my time, and not stir from Delos till all the promontories of Gyrae are clearly visible. . . .
                    (*Ad Att.*, V, 12, 1)

*To Atticus, at Rome*                    *Ephesus, late in July,* 51 B.C.
We got to Ephesus on July 22, on the 560th day after the Battle of Bovillae.[1] Our voyage was free from danger and from sea-sickness, but slower because the open Rhodian boats are so unseaworthy. About the concourse of delegations and of private individuals, and the incredible crowds that have turned out for me, first at Samos and now to a still more extraordinary degree at Ephesus, I expect you have heard, and in any case 'What's that to me?' But really, the tax-gatherers rushed to meet me as though I had come with plenary powers

1. i.e. the street-fight near Rome in which Milo killed Clodius.

and the Greeks as though I were their own Governor; from which I know you will perceive that my professions of many years are now come to the test. But I hope to be able to make good use of the training I have had from you and satisfy everyone, which will be the easier because in my province the assessment of tax has already been settled. . . .                                                    (*Ad Att.*, v, 13, 1)

*To Atticus, at Rome*                                       *Tralles, Next day*
Until I settle down somewhere, you must not expect my letters to be long, or always in my own hand. When I have time, I will guarantee both. At present we are finishing our journey on a hot and dusty road. Yesterday's letter was from Ephesus; this is from Tralles. I expect to be in my province on August 1. From that day, if you're my friend, you'll begin crossing off the days of my year of office. Meanwhile, however, I have received the following items of good news: (1) No Parthian unrest; (2) Tax-gatherers' assessments settled; (3) Soldiers' mutiny put down by Appius, and pay up to July 15 issued to them. . . .
                                                          (*Ad Att.*, v, 14, 1)

*It is vital for the political story to understand the constitutional position at this time.*

*It is not certain when Caesar's term as Governor of Gaul and the Po valley was due to end; it was probably in 50 and possibly in November. He wished to stand in 49 for the consulship for 48, and at the special request of himself and Pompey, backed by Cicero, the Senate had early in 52 granted him the special privilege of standing in absence. His election was a certainty. To be safe he had only to hang on to his army and provinces until then.*

*The Senatorial party believed that Caesar would use the consulship to overthrow the Republic. Marcellus' efforts to get him recalled on March 1, 50, having failed, their only chance was to detach Pompey from him by playing on his jealousy, and to impeach Caesar in his brief period as a private citizen* between his retirement from his provinces and army and his becoming consul-designate for 48 at the elections of 49.

*Early in 51 the Senate, without opposition from Pompey, who had had his own command in Spain prolonged till 47, had refused a request from Caesar for a short prolongation of his command in Gaul.*

*To Cicero, from Caelius*                          *Rome, August 1, 51 B.C.*

... In the political sphere we had ceased to expect any fresh developments; but when the Senate met on July 22 in the Temple of Apollo and
the question of pay for Pompey's troops came up, reference was made
to that legion he lent to Caesar, and it was asked whose strength it
belonged to, and how long Pompey was letting it stay in Gaul. Pompey
was obliged to say that he would take it back, but not until some time
after the question arose and he had been heckled by his critics. Then he
was asked about the appointment of Caesar's successor, and on this
(i.e. the assignment of provinces) the vote was that Pompey should
return to the capital as soon as possible, so that the matter of the
assignment of provinces could be dealt with in his presence (he was
on the point of going to join his army at Rimini, and did go immediately
afterwards). I think the matter will come up on August 13. Presumably
either something will be decided then, or it will be a case of scandalous
obstruction by a tribune's veto. But the one thing *I'm* looking forward
to above all else is Paullus as consul-elect giving his opinion first,
because in the course of the debate Pompey gave vent to the dictum
that it was everyone's duty to obey the Senate.

I keep on reminding you about Sittius' bond: I want you to realise
that I'm very much an interested party. Also about the panthers:
please send to Cibyra for them, and have them despatched to me. By
the way, we have heard, and it is believed certain, that the King of
Alexandria has died;[1] please be sure to let me know what steps you
advise me to take, what the situation in that Kingdom is, and who is
acting as Regent.                               (*Ad Fam.*, VIII, 4, 4)


*To Atticus*                                  *Laodicea, August 3, 51 B.C.*

I got to Laodicea on July 31. Notch up the days of my year of office
from that date. I received as warm and enthusiastic a welcome as
could be; but it's incredible how bored I am with the whole business,
what inadequate scope I have for my well-known mental drive and how
unproductive my famous energy has become. Good God! Am I to
sit in the courthouse at Laodicea, while Aulus Plotius sits at Rome?
And when our friend Caesar has that huge army, am I to have merely
a couple of skeleton legions to my credit? In any case, those are not
the things I want. The big world, the public stage, the Metropolis, my

1. Ptolemy, King of Egypt. See p. 53.

home, all of you—that is what I want. But I will bear it as best I can
so long as it's only for a year. If my term is prolonged, it's the end.
But that can easily be resisted, if only you are at Rome.

What am I doing with myself here? Damn me if I'm not spending a
fortune. It's wonderful how I'm enjoying this course of action. And
your lessons have made me so admirably innocent of plunder that I'm
afraid I may have to borrow to pay off the draft you gave me. I avoid
opening the wounds which my predecessor Appius inflicted on the
province, but they are palpable and cannot be concealed.

I am writing this on August 3, on my way from Laodicea to my
camp in Lycaonia. From there I'm thinking of going up to the Taurus
mountains, to operate against the brigand Moeragenes and settle the
matter of your runaway slave, if I can:

> Talk about an ox with panniers:
> clearly this is not my job.

But I'll put up with that, if only, please, you'll see it's not for more
than a year. Be there at the right moment, to stir up the whole Senate.

It's extraordinary how bothered I am at being out of touch for so
long. So, as I told you before, keep me informed about everything,
and especially about the political situation. I know it will take a long
time for this to reach you, but I'm entrusting it to a friend, a member
of my household, Gaius Andronicus of Pozzuoli. There will be
frequent opportunities for you to send to me, care of the Commissioners for Revenue and Harbour Dues in my jurisdiction, by the
tax-gatherers' bag.                                        (*Ad Att.*, v, 15)

*To Atticus, at Rome*               *In camp, Synnas, August,* 51 B.C.
Although the tax-gatherers' messengers are leaving while I am on
the march, and indeed at this moment on the road, I think I must
snatch a few minutes to show you that I haven't forgotten your
injunction, so I'm sitting down by the roadside to write you a line
about things which really call for a longer disquisition.

I must tell you that I have now arrived, on July 31, eagerly awaited
by all, in a province devastated and clearly irretrievably ruined. I
stayed three days at Laodicea, three at Apamea, and three also at
Synnas. Everywhere I heard the same story: the impossibility of

paying the poll-tax ordered, collection of arrears everywhere farmed out, wailing and lamentation from communities, and unheard-of cruelties that suggest not a man, but some wild beast. In fact they no longer have the will to live. However, it is a relief to the wretched communities that they are incurring no expense either on me or my staff or my quaestor or anyone. I may tell you that not only are we declining to accept the forage or whatever is usually provided under Caesar's Law, but no one is taking even firewood or anything except a roof and four beds; and in many places we forego even the roof, and camp out as often as not. As a result there is an incredible rush to greet us, from fields, from villages, from every house. I do declare that on my mere arrival they are beginning to lift up their heads, and all because of the justice and forbearance and kindness of your old friend Cicero; it surpasses anything expected.

Appius, on hearing of my approach, bolted off to the furthest corner of the province, right to Tarsus; there he's holding assizes. No news of the Parthians, but people coming from Syria say that our cavalry have been cut to pieces by bedouins. Bibulus has not even now got so far as thinking of going to his province. They say his reason is that he wants to retire from it as late as possible. I am hurrying on to my camp, two days' journey away.

*(Ad Att.,* v, 16)

*Appius Claudius, Cicero's predecessor, was a brother of Clodius. Cicero, torn as usual between sympathy with his provincials and the expediencies of home politics, refused to break permanently with this brute, who was unfortunately the father-in-law of Pompey's eldest son and Brutus; but he undid his unjust acts.*

*To Appius, at Tarsus*                    *Iconium, August 29,* 51 B.C.

When I compare my behaviour with yours, I am far more satisfied with mine, though in preserving good relations between us I am doing you as good a turn as myself. While I was at Brindisi I asked Phania, thinking his attachment to you to be obvious and knowing the place he held in your esteem, to what part of the province he considered you would like me to proceed first when I came to take over from you. When he answered that I could not please you better than by sailing to Side, although arrival there was less dignified and in many ways less convenient for me, I told him I would do so. Later, at Corfu, I met Lucius Clodius, a man so close to you that in talking to him I felt I was talking to yourself, and told him I would arrange to come first of all to the region indicated by Phania. But he thereupon, after thanking me, earnestly begged me to go straight to Laodicea, saying that you wanted to be on the nearest fringe of the province, so as to get away as soon as possible, and added that, had I not been such a successor as you would wish to meet, you would have planned to leave before your successor arrived; and this certainly bore out the letter I received at Rome, in which I thought I discerned how keen you were to get away. I answered Clodius that I would comply, far more willingly indeed than if I had had to do what I promised Phania. So I changed my plans, and sent you a letter at once, written in my own hand; and I gather from your letter that it reached you in good time. With this behaviour of mine I can find no fault: it could hardly have been friendlier.

Now turn and consider yours. Not only were you not at the place where you could meet me soonest, but you went off to a place where I could not catch you up even in the thirty days prescribed by Sulla's Law, if I am not mistaken, as the limit for overlapping. Hence your actions seem to people who do not know on what terms we are to be those of a stranger, to put it very mildly, and of one trying to avoid a meeting, while mine seem those of a very close and intimate friend. Yet before I got to the province I received a letter from you in which, while you did indicate that you were setting out for Tarsus, you held out definite hopes of meeting me. Meanwhile certain persons, ill-disposed no doubt (for this is a palpable and widespread trait), but not lacking plausible grounds for their gossip, in their ignorance of my loyalty to you, were trying to alienate me from you by saying that you were holding assizes at Tarsus, making various decisions, issuing decrees and delivering judgements, although you had every reason to suppose that you had been already superseded—actions generally avoided even by those who expect they are shortly going to be relieved. I took no notice of their talk, and indeed, believe me, I thought of any action you were taking as so much trouble the less for me, and I was glad that my governorship of a year, which was too long for my liking, should be whittled down to hardly more than eleven months by one month's work being taken off my shoulders in my absence. But, frankly, one thing does upset me, that, with troops so scarce, three cohorts, and those the strongest, are absent, and I do not know where they are. I am also very much worried by not knowing where I shall see you, and I put off writing to you because I was expecting daily to see you; meanwhile I have had no letter from you to let me know what you were doing or where I should see you. So I have sent you an able officer whom I have every reason to trust, Decimus Antonius, commander of the reserve, to whom you may please to hand over the cohorts, so that I can get something done while the time of year is still favourable. I was encouraged by our friendship and by your letter to hope that I might have the advantage of your advice in this matter, and even now I have not given up hope. But the truth is, that unless you write to me, I can have no notion when or where I shall see you.

For my part, I shall be at pains to convince people both well- and ill-disposed that I am on the best of terms with you. You seem to have given the ill-disposed some grounds for thinking otherwise about your feelings towards me. If you will put that right, I shall be very much obliged. To enable you to calculate where you can meet me without transgressing Sulla's Law: I entered the province on July 31; I am travelling to Cilicia via Cappadocia; and I am moving my camp from Iconium on August 31. It is now for you, if you think it your duty to meet me, to decide, on the basis of the above dates and itinerary, what will be the most convenient time and place. (*Ad Fam.*, III, 6)

*To Cicero, from Caelius*                    Rome, September 2, 51 B.C.
. . . In nearly all my letters I have mentioned the panthers.[1] It will be a disgrace to you if, while Patiscus has sent Curio ten panthers, you do not send a great many more. Those ten, and ten others from Africa, Curio has presented to me, so you need not think he only gives away country houses. If only you'll remember and send for some from Cibyra, and also from Pamphylia (where they tell me more are caught), you'll get what you want. I am all the more exercised about it now because I think I shall have to make all the preparations without my colleague. For old friendship's sake, do make yourself do this. You always like taking trouble, as much as I hate it. The only trouble this business entails is speaking a few words, that is, giving the

1. Caelius wanted these for a show he would be expected to give as aedile.

necessary orders; for once they are caught, the people I have sent about Sittius' bond will be available to feed and transport them. I think also that, if you hold out any hopes in your letters, I will send out some more people. . . .                                                            (*Ad Fam.*, VIII, 9, 3)

*On September 30 the Senate passed a resolution that the consuls for the year 50 should raise the question of a successor to Caesar's provinces on the earliest date consonant with tradition, March 1. But there were two snags—either Caesar might find a tribune to obstruct any decision by his veto, or he might claim his special privilege of standing for the consulship for 49 in absence, and so retain his command until, as consul-designate, he was immune from impeachment.*

*To Cicero, from Caelius*                                         *Rome, October,* 51 B.C.
. . . Certain words let fall by Pompey have caused comment, and greatly reassured people: he said that it would be out of order for him to give a decision on Caesar's provinces before March 1, but that after that date he would have no hesitation. On being asked, 'What if someone should interpose a veto at that time?' he replied that it made no odds whether Caesar openly refused to obey the Senate or suborned someone to obstruct its procedure. When someone else asked, 'What if he wants to be consul and still keep his army?' he replied, ever so mildly, 'What if my own son wants to take a stick to me?' Such utterances convinced people that Pompey is having words with Caesar. So now, as far as I can see, Caesar is willing to climb down so far as to accept one of two alternatives: either to stay where he is, and not have his name put forward for the consulship this year,[1] or, if he can first secure his election, to give up his province.

Curio[2] is preparing to oppose him tooth and nail; I don't know how far he can succeed. One thing seems clear, that a man of sound views, even if he achieves nothing, is safe from falling. As for me, Curio is treating me generously, and his generosity is involving me in some trouble; for if he hadn't given me the beasts he got over from Africa for his show, we could have done without panthers; as it is, since I must exhibit them, please take pains, as I'm always asking you,

1. Presumably in 50, for the year 49.
2. Now tribune.

to let us have something in the way of beasts from where you are; and
don't forget Sittius' bond. . . .                    (*Ad Fam.*, VIII, 8, 9–10)

*To Caelius, at Rome*          *Before Pindenissus, November* 14, 51 B.C.

Just see how your letters fail to reach me: nothing can induce me
to believe that you haven't written to me since you were elected aedile,
especially when you had two pieces of news so important and worthy
of congratulations, about yourself because it was what I was hoping,
about Hillus[1] (excuse my lisp!) because it was a surprise; and yet I
assure you I have got no letter from you since that splendid election,
which made me wild with joy, so I fear the same fate may have befallen
some of my letters to you. I have never posted a single letter home
without sending one to you with it, and there is nothing in the world
so dear and precious to me as you are. But let's drop the lisp and
return to business.

Your wish has come true; for you wished me only so much trouble
as would qualify me for triumphal laurels. You are afraid of the
Parthians because you mistrust the strength of our forces. Well, this
is how things have turned out. As soon as the outbreak of war with
the Parthians was announced, relying on certain difficulties of the
terrain and on the configuration of the mountains, I moved up to
Amanus an army which was respectably reinforced with auxiliaries,
and also, if I may say so, by the prestige of my name among people
to whom I was only a name. For one often hears in these parts, 'Is this
the man to whom the city owes . . . ? On whom the Senate . . . ?'—
you know how it goes on. By the time I got to Amanus, a mountain
whose watershed divides my territory from Bibulus', our Cassius, to
my great delight, had successfully repulsed the enemy from Antioch,
and Bibulus had taken over his province. Meanwhile with all my
forces I harassed the Amanians, chronic enemies of ours. Many were
killed or captured, the rest scattered, their strongholds surprised and
burnt down. So, after being hailed as 'Imperator' on the strength of a
victory that qualified me for this honour,[2] at Issus (the place where,
you have often told me, Clitarchus informs you that Alexander

1. i.e. Hirrus, who could not pronounce his 'r's; he was an enemy of Cicero,
and Caelius' rival for the aedileship.

2. The soldiers conferred it by acclamation. The Cassius mentioned is the
future conspirator against Caesar.

defeated Darius), I transported my army into the most seditious region of Cilicia. There I have been for twenty-five days now, besieging the highly fortified town of Pindenissus with ramps, penthouses and towers, with such resources and such trouble, that I feel there is nothing lacking in my battle-honours save the name of this town. If I take it, as I trust I shall,[1] it will then be time to send an official despatch. . . .                                      (*Ad Fam.*, II, 10, 1–3)

*To Cicero, from Caelius*                              *Rome, February,* 50 B.C.

The news has doubtless reached you that Appius has been impeached by Dolabella; but I must confess I expected more prejudice against him. Appius in fact did quite an astute thing: as soon as Dolabella began proceedings, he entered the capital, and thereby renounced his candidature for a Triumph.[2] By so doing he took the edge off people's talk, and showed himself readier than his accuser had anticipated. He now sets his hopes mainly on you. I'm sure you don't really hate him. It is in your power to put him under an obligation to you to any extent you choose. You would be more free to act in the whole affair if you had never been on bad terms with him. As it is, if you press your full legal rights according to 'the strictest standards of conduct', you will have to beware of giving the impression that your reconciliation to him was not quite candid or sincere. On the other hand, it will be quite safe for you to show him any favour you like in this matter, since no one could suggest that you were being deterred from doing your duty by any partiality or friendship.

One thing has occurred to me, however. Between the first and second stages of the prosecution Dolabella's wife separated from him. Now I remember your parting instructions to me,[3] and I don't suppose you've forgotten what I wrote to you. This is not the time to say any more, but one piece of advice I can give you: if you view the idea with any favour, nevertheless do not show any sign of your partiality at present, but wait and see how he comes out of this trial. Think of the harm it may do you if it leaks out; and further, if any hint of it escapes

1. He took it after 57 days, and based his claim to a Triumph on this.

2. He was accused probably of treason, and acquitted with help from Cicero. Candidates for the coveted honour of a Triumph (procession with captives through Rome) were not allowed to enter the city previously.

3. Presumably to look out for a suitable husband for Tullia, now divorced from Crassipes.

meanwhile, what undignified and inopportune publicity it will receive. Dolabella will be unable to keep his mouth shut about something which has turned up so opportunely for his schemes, and which will shed so much more lustre on him at the time when he is conducting the prosecution, especially as he is the sort of person who could hardly hold his tongue about such a matter even if it were disastrous to him to let it out.

Pompey is said to be working hard for Appius, so much so that they think he will send one or other of his sons to see you. We always acquit people here, and, God knows, everything shameful and discreditable is most carefully screened. Our consuls set a fine example of energy: so far the only decree they have managed to get through the Senate is the routine one fixing the date of the Latin Festival. Curio's tribunate is a complete frost. But words cannot describe how flat everything is here. If I wasn't having a fight with the shop-keepers and water commissioners, the political machine would have sunk into complete stagnation. The Parthians may not be keeping you warm, but here we're frozen stiff. However, Heaven knows how, even without the Parthians' help, Bibulus has managed to lose the odd battalion in the Amanus area, so it's reported.

P.S.—I said that Curio is having a frost; well now he's having a very warm time indeed; in fact he is being roasted and made mincemeat. Quite capriciously, because he failed in the matter of the leap-month,[1] he has gone over to the People's Party, and is beginning to make speeches in favour of Caesar. He is ostentatiously promoting a Road Bill somewhat analogous to Rullus' Land Bill, and a Foodstuffs Bill making the aediles responsible for weights and measures. This has happened since I wrote the above.

Do please, if you do anything for Appius, let me have some of the credit. As to Dolabella, I advise you to hold your hand. You ought to do so out of consideration for the reasons I mentioned, and for your own dignity and reputation for fair dealing.

It will be a disgrace to you if you don't get me my panthers from Cibyra.                                     (*Ad Fam.*, VIII, 6)

---

1. To correct the calendar; this should have been inserted on this occasion after Feb. 23, 50; but, like so much else, it was a political pawn. The poet Lucan, looking back 100 years later, thought that Curio's defection turned the scale. It was bought for a huge sum.

*To Appius*                                    *Laodicea, February,* 50 B.C.

At long last a letter worthy of Appius Claudius, full of kindness, courtesy and thoughtfulness! Clearly the sight of civilisation has revived your old civility. For I had been very sorry to read the letters you sent on your journey home, before you left Asia, one about my not letting the envoys start,[1] and the other about my holding up the building project of the people of Appia[2]; so I wrote back a little huffily, conscious as I was of my continual goodwill towards you. When I read the letter you entrusted to my freed man Philotimus, I perceived and realised that there were many in the province who wished we had feelings towards one another different from those we have, whereas when you approached the capital, or rather as soon as you saw your own people, you found out from them how loyal to you I had been in your absence, and how keen and scrupulous in carrying out my obligations towards you. So you can imagine how much store I set by the remark in your letter, that should anything go wrong in the matter of my distinction (very unlikely, but still—), you would do me a like service in return; and you will have no difficulty in doing so, for goodwill and friendship (or may I say, affection?) can accomplish anything.

For my part, though my own judgement and letters from many friends led me to expect it, I was delighted at the high hopes and indeed practical certainty of your obtaining your Triumph which were expressed in your letter, not because I thought it made it easier for me to obtain one (that would be too like Epicurean utilitarianism), but frankly because your honour and eminence are in themselves near my heart. So since you hear of more people setting out for this province than others do, because nearly all of them call on you to ask if there is anything they can do for you, I should be most grateful if you would write to me as soon as your expectation and my earnest desire is fulfilled. . . .                                  (*Ad Fam.*, III, 9, 1–2)

---

1. To save the provincials expense, Cicero discouraged them from voting public funds to send to Rome the usual delegation of compliment to the retiring governor unless they really wanted to, which annoyed Appius. Nevertheless he hoped to retain Appius' support for his claim to a Triumph.

2. A number of the citizens had complained of the taxes necessitated by this project which Appius had sanctioned.

*Shakespeare's Plutarchian Brutus professed himself above wringing 'from the hard hands of peasants their vile trash'. It is worth while, in spite of the complicated details involved, to let Cicero tell the following story; it shows him struggling for his conscience against the claims of expediency and the promptings even of Atticus.*

*To Atticus, in N.W. Greece*      *Laodicea, February 13, 50 B.C.*

... Now let me tell you about Brutus. Among the acquaintances of your friend Brutus are two creditors of the community of Salamis in Cyprus named Marcus Scaptius and Publius Matinius, whom he recommended to me warmly. Matinius I have not met, but Scaptius came to see me in camp. I promised that for Brutus' sake I would see that the Salaminians paid up. He thanked me, and asked for the post of prefect there. I replied, in accordance with what I told you, that I never gave such a post to a business man. This rule I had already justified to Pompey, when he made a similar request for someone, not to mention Torquatus in the case of your friend Laenius, and many others. But I added that if it was only in order to get his bond paid that he wanted the post, I would take steps myself to see that he got satisfaction. He thanked me, and took his leave. Now our friend Appius had given this Scaptius a few squadrons of cavalry with which to put pressure on the Salaminians, and had also treated him as prefect. Scaptius was oppressing them. I ordered the cavalry to leave Cyprus, and this annoyed him.

To cut a long story short, in order to keep my word to him, when he came, along with the Salaminians, to see me at Tarsus, I told them to pay up. They were full of complaints about the bond, and about Scaptius' outrages. I said I was deaf to that. I advised them, I even begged them in return for my kindness to their community, to finish the business. Finally I said I would compel them. The fellows then not merely did not refuse, but even said they were really paying out of my pocket, for inasmuch as I had not accepted what they usually had to give a governor, in a sense they were paying at my expense, and even paying somewhat less on Scaptius' account than they normally did in governor's dues. I expressed my appreciation. 'Right', says Scaptius, 'let's reckon up the amount.' Now although my inaugural edict fixed the rate of interest at 12 per cent compound interest reckoned by the year (not by the month), he was demanding 48 per cent under the terms of his bond. 'What?' I said; 'How can I go against my own edict?' Then he produced a decree passed by the Senate in the year 56, binding any governor of Cilicia to honour that bond. At first I was aghast: it meant ruin to the community. Then I discovered two senatorial decrees of the same year about that very bond. When the Salaminians wanted to raise a loan at Rome, they were unable to do so because of Gabinius' Law against lending to provincials. But friends of Brutus, relying on his influence, agreed to lend at 48 per cent, on condition they were covered by a special decree of the Senate. So through Brutus' influence a rider was passed: 'This decree shall not apply to the Salaminians and those who have lent money to them,' and the money changed hands. It afterwards occurred to the lenders that this rider was valueless, because under Gabinius' Law no such bond could be enforced at law; so another rider was passed, that this particular bond should be good at law. It follows that this bond was now on exactly the same footing as any other.

When I had given this ruling, Scaptius took me aside. He said he had nothing to say against it, but that the Salaminians estimated the principal of their debt at 200 talents. This sum he was anxious to get, though actually they owed a little less. He asked me to induce them to make it 200. 'Very good,' I said. Then I sent Scaptius out, and called them in. 'What about you?' I said; 'What do you think you owe?' '106 talents',[1] they replied. I put this to Scaptius. The fellow began to bluster. 'Very well,' I said; 'All you need do is compare accounts.' Down they sit, do their sums, and find that they come out exactly the same. The Salaminians were eager to pay, and urged him to accept their offer. Scaptius took me aside again, and asked me to let the matter stand over;—an impertinent request, but I consented; and I also rejected the protesting Salaminians' application for leave to deposit the money in a temple treasury. Everyone present exclaimed that Scaptius was the height of impudence for not being content with 12 per cent compound interest, and some that he was the height of folly. To me he seemed more impudent than foolish. For either he was not content with 12 per cent on good security, or he was hoping to get 48 per cent on risky security.[2]

There's my case. If Brutus doesn't approve, I can't see why we

---

1. i.e. as to the principal: the rate of interest remained in dispute.
2. Through a less scrupulous governor than Cicero.

should be friends with him. But his uncle Cato will, I know, approve, especially as the Senate has recently passed a decree (since you left, I think) fixing the rate for money-lenders at 12 per cent simple interest. Knowing your skill at ready reckoning, I've no doubt you've already calculated the difference. . . .

Think how to put my case against Brutus—if you can speak of a 'case' when there is nothing that can honestly be pleaded on the other side, especially as I have left the matter entirely unprejudiced for my successor. . . . (*Ad Att.*, V, 21, 10–13)

*To Atticus*                 *Laodicea, February* 24, 50 B.C.

. . . Now let me tell you about the Salaminian affair, which I gather came as a surprise to you no less than to me. Brutus never told me the money was really *his*. I actually have his memorandum-book in which it says: 'The Salaminians owe money to my friends Scaptius and Matinius.' It was they that he recommended to me, adding as a spur to my zeal that he had gone security for them for a large sum. I had settled that they should be paid at 12 per cent compound interest for two years; whereas Scaptius was demanding 48 per cent. I was afraid that, if I yielded to him, you yourself would drop me; for I should have gone back on my own edict, and utterly ruined a community dependent on the good faith of its patron, Cato, and of Brutus himself, and distinguished by favours from me; when lo and behold, Scaptius thrusts into my hands a letter from Brutus saying that he himself is the party concerned, which he had never said before either to you or to me. He even asks me to give Scaptius the prefecture. Now on your advice I had expressly made the rule, no prefectures for business men; and if I did make any exception, it would not be for this fellow; for he had been prefect under Appius and even had some squadrons of cavalry, which he used to besiege the local Senate in their Senate-house at Salamis, with the result that five members died of hunger; in consequence of which, on the first day I set foot in the province, since envoys from Cyprus had already come to meet me at Ephesus, I sent orders for the cavalry to leave the island at once. For this reason Scaptius, as I believe, sent letters to Brutus criticising me unjustly.

However, this is my attitude, that if Brutus thinks I ought to have made the rate 48 per cent, when I was keeping it to 12 per cent through-

out the province, and had fixed it at this by edict with the acquiescence
of even the most grasping money-lenders, and if he complains that I
did not give a command to a business man, a course which I succeeded
in justifying both to our friend Torquatus in the case of Laenius and
to Pompey himself in the case of Statius, and if he is annoyed at the
withdrawal of the cavalry—then I shall be sorry that he should be
angry with me, but far more sorry that he is not the man I thought he
was. One thing Scaptius will have to admit: that under my award he
had the chance of recovering the whole sum without breaking my
edict. Not only that (and here I'm afraid you yourself may disapprove),
but the interest should by rights have ceased to accumulate; for the
Salaminians were willing to deposit the money in a temple at the rate
of interest fixed by my edict, but I managed to persuade them not to
raise this point. To me they conceded this, but what will happen if my
successor is Brutus' brother-in-law, Paullus?

All this I have done for the sake of Brutus, who may have written
you the kindest letters about me, but always writes to me, even when
asking a favour, in a haughty, arrogant and uncompromising tone.
Would you be so kind as to write to him about all this, to find out for
me how he is taking it, and then let me know?

I am well aware that I told you all about this in a previous letter, but
I wanted to make it quite clear to you that I have not forgotten your
remark in one of your letters, that it is quite sufficient for me if I carry
away from this province nothing else but Brutus' goodwill. Very well,
if you will have it so; but provided, I assume, that I can do so with a
clear conscience. Accordingly I have given my ruling, that Scaptius
has been duly and lawfully paid; on the equity of this you yourself
will be able to judge, and I need not appeal to a Cato. But don't
imagine that I have thrown your injunction to the winds: it is fixed
in my heart of hearts. With tears in your eyes you begged me to
remember my good name. Have you ever written to me without
mentioning this? So let who will be angry, I will put up with that; for
I prefer to be on good terms with my conscience, especially now that I
have given bail for my good conduct with my six books of *The
Republic*, of which I am very glad to hear you approve. . . .

Caelius has sent me one of his freedmen with a carefully worded
letter about panthers and about communities' contributions. I have
replied, that I am sorry to find that I am in such outer darkness that

news has not reached Rome that in my province no contributions are exacted except in payment of debts, and explained to him that it is impossible either for me to solicit or for him to receive any subscription to his show. I have also warned him, much as I love him, that after accusing others he should walk more circumspectly himself, and that as to the other point, it is inconsistent with my good reputation that there should be a public panther-hunt under my jurisdiction. . . .

(Ad Att., VI, I, 5–8; 21)

To Caelius, at Rome                          Laodicea, April 4, 50 B.C.

Would you ever have believed that words could fail <i>me</i>, and not merely such words as you orators use, but this homely jargon of ours. But so it is, and the reason is my extraordinary anxiety over what will be decreed about the provinces. I have a strange longing for the capital, an incredible longing for my friends, and for you as much as any; and I am so sick of the province, either because I seem to have established such a reputation that there is now less chance of its being enhanced than of some reverse of fortune, or because the whole business is unworthy of my powers, inasmuch as I both can and often do sustain much greater responsibilities in the State; or because the threat of a major war is hanging over me, and I think I shall escape it if I am relieved by the day appointed.

About the panthers, energetic steps are being taken on my instructions by those who regularly hunt them; but there is a remarkable scarcity, and they say that such as there are complain bitterly that no traps are laid for anyone in my province but them; so they are reported to have decided to emigrate to Caria. However, great efforts are being made, especially by Patiscus. Any products shall be yours, but what they will amount to I have no idea. I assure you I have your aedileship very much at heart, and I am reminded of it by today's date, this being the festival of the Great Mother.

Please write to me very carefully about the political situation, as I shall place most reliance on what I hear from you.

(Ad Fam., II, 11)

To Atticus                                 Laodicea, early May, 50 B.C.

. . . I see you are pleased at my moderation and forbearance; you would be still more so, if you were here. During this very session, which I have been holding at Laodicea from February 13 to May 1 for all the Departments save Cilicia proper, I have done wonders; so many communities have been entirely freed from debt, and many others considerably relieved of it; all have enjoyed their own laws and courts, obtained home rule and come to life again. There are two ways in which I have enabled them to get rid of debts, either partly or altogether: firstly my government has involved them in no expense at all—I mean it, literally, not so much as a farthing. It is incredible how this alone has raised their heads above water. Secondly, the peculations of the Greeks themselves, their own officials, within the communities were astonishing. I questioned those who had held office during the last ten years, and they openly admitted it. So without any public scandal they took upon themselves the burden of repayment. What's more, the communities have now, without a murmur, paid the tax-gatherers, who had hitherto received nothing for the current period, the arrears even of the previous one. So I am the apple of the tax-gatherers' eye. ('Such nice, grateful people!' you'll say. Yes, I know that from experience!)

In other respects too the people have found my administration lenient and remarkably informal without being incompetent. Access to me has been much freer than is usual in the case of provincials; there's no chamberlain to get past; I have been about the house before daybreak, just as when I was a candidate. This has been welcome and a great thing for them, while for me it has been no burden so far, thanks to the training I had for those old battles of mine. . . .

(Ad Att., VI, 2, 4–5)

*Cicero had asked the Senate in April to decree a Thanksgiving Service to the gods for his successful campaign. Cato voted against this, proposing instead a vote of thanks to Cicero himself for the wisdom and integrity of his governorship; but the Senate decreed the Thanksgiving.*

*To Cicero, from Cato*                                    Rome, May, 50 B.C.
It is a pleasure to me to do what both public interest and private friendship dictate, and rejoice that the courage, integrity and devotion you displayed as a statesman in a great crisis at home are now being employed by you no less energetically as a commander abroad. Therefore what I could conscientiously do—indicate by speech and vote my

appreciation that you have defended your province by your integrity and prudence, saved the kingdom and person of King Ariobarzanes, and won back the loyalty of our allies to our rule—that I did.

As to the Thanksgiving Service decreed, if you yourself prefer that, in a matter in which the interests of the State were secured without any element of chance by your own consummate resource and self-restraint, we should render thanks to the immortal gods rather than give you the credit, I am glad of it. If, however, you are under the impression that a Thanksgiving is an earnest of a Triumph, and for that reason prefer that the credit should go to good luck[1] rather than to yourself, I must tell you that a Triumph does not invariably follow a Thanksgiving, and that it is a much finer thing than a Triumph for the Senate to decide that a province has been retained and conserved by the leniency and integrity of its commander than by military force or by the favour of Heaven; and that was the opinion I expressed when giving my vote.

My reason for writing this to you at such length, contrary to my custom, is my particular desire that you should believe in my anxiety to persuade you that, while I did what I thought was most complimentary and most consonant with your dignity, I yet rejoice that what you preferred was done.

I send you my best wishes, and trust I have yours. Continue as you have begun, and put your strict devotion to duty at the service of our allies and our State.                              (*Ad Fam.*, XV, 5)

*To Caelius, at Rome*                    *In Cilicia, June*, 50 B.C.
I'm worried about the state of affairs in Rome: news has come of such rowdy elections and such a disturbed Spring Vacation. I have not yet heard of anything further, but nothing bothered me more than that, amid all these disturbances, I was not there to share a laugh with you over anything there was to laugh at. There were many things, of course, but not such as I dare commit to writing. Another worry—I have had no letter from you about all this; and that is why, although by the time you get this I shall have already completed my year of office, I should still like a letter from you to meet me on my way home and brief me on the whole political situation, so that I shall not feel a country cousin when I arrive. No one can do this better than you.

1. Equated by Cato with the gods; cf. our expression 'Act of God'.

Your nice quiet friend Diogenes has gone off to Pessinus with Philo. They are on their way to visit Adiatorix,[1] though they are well aware that there is no prospect of either welcome or profit. The capital, my dear Caelius, the capital! Stay *there*, and enjoy a place in the sun. All residence abroad (of this I have been convinced ever since I grew up) is dim and sordid for those whose public services at Rome can bring them lustre. I only wish that, well knowing this, I had had the courage of my convictions. All the fruits of a province are not, to my mind, to be compared with a single short walk or talk with you. I trust I have gained a reputation for integrity; but that I had gained no less by refusing a province before than by conserving one now. My hopes of a Triumph? It would be triumph enough for me not to be separated so long from all I love most. However, all being well, I shall be seeing you before long. Do send a letter worthy of you to meet me.                                                   (*Ad Fam.*, II, 12)

*To Atticus, in N.W. Greece*                       *In Cilicia, June*, 50 B.C.
I have no fresh news for you since the letter I handed to your freedman Philogenes, but I must send you a line, as I am sending Philotimus back to Rome.

First, my chief worry at the moment—not that you can help me at all, since the matter is already upon me, and you are at the back of beyond:

> Wide seas betwixt us lie,
> Where countless waves before the south wind fly.

The day draws near, as you see (for I am due to leave my province on July 30), and still no successor! Whom can I leave in charge? Common sense and public opinion indicate my brother, firstly because it is a position of honour, so he should have the refusal, and secondly because I have no one else of praetorian standing; for Pomptinus has already left me according to the terms of his contract (he came out only on that condition). My quaestor no one thinks suitable: he is irresponsible, immoral and light-fingered. But my brother presents an immediate obstacle: I doubt if I can persuade him. He hates provincial life, and hateful it is, God knows, and a frightful bore.

1. Son of the Tetrarch of Galatia. Possibly Diogenes was to be his tutor.

And then, supposing he does not like to refuse me, what is my duty to him? Considering that they think there is a war on in Syria, and on a large scale, and that probably it will break out into this province, where there is no proper garrison and only the annually voted supplies, wouldn't it seem unbrotherly to leave a brother in charge, and yet irresponsible to leave a nobody? So you see I am suffering from a heavy anxiety, and am badly in need of advice. In fact, I could have gladly done without the whole business. How much better your 'province' is: you can leave whenever you like—perhaps you have left already; and you can put anyone you like in charge of Thesprotia or Chaonia! I have yet to meet Quintus, and find out, supposing I decide to ask him, whether I can get him to consent; and supposing I can, I am still not clear what I want. . . .          (*Ad Att.*, VI, 3, 1–2)

*For several months Curio's tribunician veto had prevented discussion of a successor to Caesar, but Pompey and the Senate were united in insisting that he should leave his provinces and army as soon as the legal term of his command was reached.*

*To Cicero, from Caelius*                    *Rome, June,* 50 B.C.
   . . . As for politics in general, all controversy centres on one issue, the provinces; and on this Pompey seems so far to have thrown his weight on the side of the Senate, to the effect that Caesar should retire on November 13. Curio is determined to allow anything rather than that. All his other schemes he has thrown to the winds. Our friends, of course (you know who I mean), don't dare bring the matter to a crisis.

   This is how the stage is set. Pompey, as though not attacking Caesar but deciding what he thinks fair to him, says that Curio is picking a quarrel. But he is strongly against, and obviously fears, Caesar's being elected consul-designate before he has given up his army and province. He is having a bad time from Curio, and his whole conduct during his second consulship is being attacked. I tell you this much: if they suppress Curio on every point, Caesar will come to the help of his vetoing tribune; but if, as seems likely, they are afraid to do so, Caesar will stay on as long as he likes. . . .
                         (*Ad Fam.*, VIII, 11, 3)

D

*To Cicero, from Caelius*                          *Rome, June,* 50 B.C.

I congratulate you on forming a connection[1] with a man who is, I swear, first rate: that's my opinion of him. Those traits which hitherto have made him his own worst enemy he has now shaken off with maturity. If any remain, I am confident they will quickly vanish through your presence and influence and Tullia's refinement; for he is not obstinate in his faults, nor too thick to see the better path. And, last but not least, I'm very fond of him.

You will be glad to hear, my dear Cicero, that our friend Curio's veto regarding the provinces had excellent results. For when the question of the veto was discussed (as was obligatory under a decree of the Senate), and Marcellus spoke first to the effect that the tribunes should be negotiated with, a crowded House voted in exactly the opposite sense. The fact is that Pompey the 'Great' is in such a state of enervation, that he can hardly make up his own mind what he wants. The Senate had come over to the view that they should consider the candidature for the consulship of a man who was unwilling to give up either his army or his provinces. How Pompey takes this, I will let you know as soon as I can discover. What manner of Republic we shall have if he either resists by force or remains apathetic, will be the concern of you old plutocrats.[2]

As I write this, Hortensius[3] is breathing his last.

(*Ad Fam.,* VIII, 13)

*To Caelius, at Rome*                          *Side, early August,* 50 B.C.

... The political outlook worries me a lot: as for Curio, I wish him well; as for Caesar, all honour to him; as for Pompey, I could die for him; but what I really love is the Republic; and as for you, you are not doing much about her; you seem to me to be torn between being a good friend and a good patriot.

On leaving my province I put my quaestor, your namesake Caelius, in command. 'What! A mere boy?' Yes; but he is my quaestor; he is a young man of good birth; and I followed an almost unbroken precedent. Besides, there was no one who had held higher office to put in charge; Pomptinus had left long ago; my brother Quintus could not

1. Tullia had become engaged to Dolabella, who was probably not yet 20.
2. Who would be skinned by the Caesarian People's Party.
3. Cicero's chief rival at the bar.

be induced to consent (and if I had left him, the malicious would be saying that I had not in fact carried out the wishes of the Senate and left my province after a year, since I had left my other self behind; perhaps they would add that the Senate's intention was that only men who had not been governors before should govern provinces, whereas my brother had been Governor of West Asia Minor for three years). Anyhow, I am now rid of my anxieties, whereas if I had left my brother, I should have been in a constant state of uneasiness.[1] Finally, it was not on my own initiative, but according to a precedent set by the two most powerful people in the State, who gladly took up anyone of the name of Cassius or Antonius, that—well, I was not so much anxious to conciliate as anxious not to alienate a young man of good birth. You must needs applaud my decision, for it cannot now be altered. . . .                    (*Ad Fam.*, II, 15, 3–4)

*To Atticus*                  *Rhodes, about August* 10, 50 B.C.

While in my province I was paying every mark of respect to Appius, I suddenly found myself the father-in-law of his accuser Dolabella! 'Heaven's blessing on the match!' you say; and so say I, and know you are sincere. But, believe me, it came as a complete surprise to me; indeed, I had sent trusted messengers to Terentia and Tullia about Tiberius Nero, who had made a proposal to me, but they arrived at Rome to find Tullia already engaged. However, I hope this will turn out better; any any rate, I understand the two are delighted with the young man's good manners and affability. So, for the rest, please don't pick holes. . . .                    (*Ad Att.*, VI, 6, 1)

*To Cato, at Rome*                    *Rhodes, August,* 50 B.C.

'Glad I am to have the praises of a man so praised as thou', as Hector says, I think, in Naevius; and pleasant indeed is praise that comes from men who have themselves enjoyed it all their lives. I can assure you that with the congratulations you sent me and the declaration you made when voting in the Senate I have attained the summit of my ambitions. And this was to me both the most complimentary and the most gratifying feature, that you willingly conceded to friendship what you could conscientiously concede to truth. Even if our State were com-

1. To Atticus Cicero confessed his real objection: Quintus' insolence and indiscretion, and his son's conceit.

posed largely or entirely of Catos (though indeed the emergence of one is a miracle), what laurels, or what triumphal car, could I compare with praise from you? For to my feeling, and in consideration of the well-known integrity and fineness of your judgement, there could be no higher eulogy than that speech of yours, a full copy of which was sent me by my friends.

But the reason for my aspiration (I will not call it desire) I have explained to you in a previous letter; and although it has seemed inadequate to you, it has this much justification, that while such an honour should not be too much coveted, yet it should by no means be despised if the Senate sees fit to confer it; and I trust that that body, in view of the services I have undertaken for the State, will not think me unworthy of such an honour, especially as its conferment would be according to precedent. If it turns out so, I shall only remind you of your own very kind words and ask you, while you have paid me what you consider the highest possible compliment by the opinion you expressed, to rejoice nevertheless if what I preferred has been done.

It is in this light that I see your actions, your feelings and your words; and your pleasure at the honour done me by the vote of a Thanksgiving Service is attested by your presence at the drafting; for I am well aware that such decrees are usually drafted by the closest friends of the man to whom the honour is being paid.

I shall, I hope, be seeing you before long. May I find the State in a better condition than I fear I shall!                    (*Ad Fam.*, xv, 6)


*To Cicero, from Caelius*                    *Rome, early August,* 50 B.C.
... With regard to high politics, I have often written to you that I can see no prospect of peace in a year's time, and the nearer the clash, which is inevitable,[1] approaches, the clearer looms the danger.

The issue over which the powers that be are going to come to blows is, that whereas Pompey is determined not to allow Caesar to become consul unless he gives up his army and provinces, Caesar is convinced that he cannot be safe once he has parted with his army. Caesar does, however, propose this compromise, that both should give up their armies. So all that show of affection and their detested alliance

1. Caelius could see no alternative to Civil War, unless either Caesar or Pompey were sent against the Parthians; but the Parthian threat receded.

is not merely degenerating into bickering behind the scenes, but breaking out into open war.

About my own position I am at a loss what to decide (and you too, no doubt, will be troubled by the same dilemma): to the Caesarians as men I am bound by ties of gratitude and friendship, while I favour the Senate's cause but hate its champions. You will of course realise that, in a case of internal dissension, men should support the side that is in the right so long as it is a matter of politics and not fighting, but the stronger side when it comes to open warfare, considering then that might is right. Now in this dispute I perceive that Pompey will have with him the Senate and the judiciary in general, while all those who have anything to fear or nothing to hope will rally to Caesar. The latter's army is incomparably the better. I only hope we have time enough to survey the forces of each, and to choose sides.[1]

I had almost forgotten the chief thing I had to tell you. Do you know, Appius as censor is showing portentous artistry. He is up in arms about statues and pictures, excessive holdings of land and debts. He has got it into his head that his censorship will act as soap and soda for him. I fancy he's mistaken. Instead of merely washing off the dirt, it's taking off his skin and exposing the raw flesh. Hurry home, for God's sake, and don't miss the chance of laughing at what's going on here—Drusus presiding over a trial for unnatural vice, and Appius worrying about pictures and statues! It's worth hurrying for, believe me. . . .                                      (*Ad Fam.*, VIII, 14, 2–4)

*To Terentia*                              *Athens, October 16, 50 B.C.*

Our darling Marcus and I send our best wishes to you and to our adored Tullia.

We reached Athens on October 14, after a slow and uncomfortable voyage with the wind against us. As we came off the ship Acastus was there to meet us with our letters, having taken only twenty-one days. Smart work! I got your letter, and gathered from it that you were afraid that previous ones might not have been delivered; but they all arrived safely, and I was most grateful for the full account you gave of everything; nor was I at all surprised at the shortness of the one Acastus brought, since you are expecting to see me—us, I should say—in person shortly; and we too are eager to be with you as soon

1. He chose Caesar's, helped probably by a bribe.

as possible, though I have no illusions about how I shall find the political situation, since I learnt from the letters of many friends, which Acastus brought, that things look like war, so that when I arrive I shall be obliged to reveal what I really think. However, since we must face things as they come, I will make all the more effort to arrive sooner, so that we can have a better chance of discussing the whole situation. If your health permits, Terentia, I should be glad if you would come as far as you can to meet me. . . .

(Ad Fam., XIV, 5, 1–2)

*To Atticus*                                      *Athens, October* 16, 50 B.C.

. . . In the name of Fortune, do devote all the affection you have lavished on me, and all your wisdom, which, God knows, I count unrivalled in every sphere, to taking stock of my whole position. For unless the same Providence who surpassed our most sanguine prayers in saving us from a Parthian war takes pity on the State, I foresee such a conflict as has never been before. True, this calamity will fall not only on me, but on everyone; it is not to this that I am asking you to give your mind, but do please tackle my own private problem. Do you realise that it was on your advice that I got involved with both Pompey and Caesar? I only wish I had listened from the outset to your most kind advice,

But never didst thou sway my heart within me.

At last, however, you persuaded me to take up with Pompey, because he had done so much for me, and with Caesar, because he was so powerful. So I did this, and did it so well by every kind of consideration that I took an unrivalled place in the affections of each. My idea was that by attaching myself to Pompey I should never be forced to do anything unconstitutional, and by agreeing with Caesar I should avoid any clash with Pompey, they were so closely allied. But now, on your own showing, and in my view as well, they are approaching a head-on collision. Each of them is counting on me:—Caesar may be only pretending; Pompey at least has no doubts, rightly supposing that his present political attitude has my warm approval. At any rate, each of them sent me a letter, which arrived with yours, from which it appeared that neither set more store by anyone than by me.

But what am I to do? I don't mean in the last resort: if it comes to open warfare, I see that it would be better to lose with Pompey than to win with Caesar. But what about the debate which will be in progress when I arrive, whether he should be allowed to stand in absence, and whether he should disband his army? 'Marcus Tullius is in possession of the house.' What am I to say? 'Please be so good as to wait till I have consulted Atticus'? No, there's no chance of evasion. Shall I speak *against* Caesar? '*Think of the vows. . . .*' When he asked me himself at Ravenna about getting Caelius, as tribune, to propose a bill enabling him to stand in his absence, I gave him my support. Himself? Yes, and Pompey too, in that wonderful third consulship of his. Shall I then speak *for* him? 'I fear reproach . . .' not only from Pompey, but from 'all the knights and dames of Troy'.

Polydamas will be the first to gird.

Polydamas? That's you, the commender of my deeds and writings. Have I avoided this trap all through the past two years, when Caesar's province has been under debate, only to stumble now into the thick of the trouble? So 'to let a fool give his opinion first', I am very much inclined to begin taking steps about my Triumph, and so have a good excuse for remaining outside the capital. And yet they will do everything they can to elicit my opinion. Don't laugh; but how I wish I were still in my province! I certainly should have done better to stay, if this was in store for me.

Still, that would have been misery too. For, *en passant*, there is one thing I want to tell you. All that show of virtue, which even you praised to the skies in your letters, proved only a veneer. Verily the path of virtue is not easy, and the path of daily hypocrisy is hard indeed! When I decided that it was right and honourable to leave for my quaestor a year's money out of the annual expenditure voted for me, and pay back a million sesterces into the Treasury, my staff complained that all that should have been distributed to them, so that I should appear more benevolent to the exchequer of Phrygians and Cilicians than to our own. I held my ground, since I valued my good name above everything. Yet there was no possible honour that I had not conferred on any of them. This is a digression, as Thucydides would say, but instructive.

But to return to my position, do consider first by what device I can retain Caesar's goodwill, and next about my Triumph, which seems, unless the political crisis gets in the way, to be in the bag, judging from my correspondence and from my Thanksgiving. For the man who voted against that, Cato, was ready to vote for more than all the Triumphs in the world; and of his two supporters one, Favonius, is a friend of mine, and the other, Hirrus, has a private grudge against me. Besides, Cato took part in the drafting, and sent me the kindest of letters about his vote. On the other hand, Caesar, in writing to congratulate me on the Thanksgiving, was jubilant over Cato's vote,[1] and without mentioning the speech that accompanied it, merely remarked that he had voted against the Thanksgiving. . . .

*(Ad Att.,* VII, 1, 2–7)

*To Tiro,*[2] *at Patras*                          *Leucas, November* 7, 50 B.C.
First let me send you best wishes from myself and Marcus, and from my brother Quintus and his son.

I read your letter with mixed feelings, being much upset by the first page, though somewhat reassured by the second. So now I have no doubt whatever that, until you are absolutely well, you must not risk travelling either by sea or land. It will be quite soon enough for me to see you, if I see you perfectly fit again. Your statement that your doctor is well thought of is confirmed by what I hear, but I must say I do not approve of the cure he prescribes. For instance, you should never have been given soup when your stomach was upset. However, I have written him a careful letter, and another to Lyso.

I have also written to that charming, kind and very attentive fellow, Curius, asking him, among other things, if you like the idea, to take you into his own house; for I'm afraid Lyso may be rather casual, firstly because all Greeks are, and secondly because he did not acknowledge my letter. But you speak well of him, so you shall decide what should be done. I only beg you, my dear Tiro, to spare no expense on anything that may be necessary for your health. I have

1. Thinking it would estrange Cicero from the Senatorial Party. A month later, when Cato voted for a Thanksgiving for his futile son-in-law Bibulus, who had merely shut himself up in Antioch, Cicero saw his present action in a more sinister light.

2. Cicero's freedman secretary, who afterwards edited his letters.

written to Curius to advance you any money you ask for. I think you should give the doctor something on account, to make him take more interest.

Your services to me have been incalculable—in my home, in the courts, in business, in my province, in matters public and private, and in my reading and writing. You will surpass them all if, as I trust, you present yourself in good health. You should, if all goes well, have a splendid journey home with my quaestor, Mescinius; he's quite agreeable, and seems very fond of you. But when you have done taking care of your health, then my dear Tiro take care over your voyage. I have not the least desire that you should hurry. My only anxiety is that you should come back safe and sound. . . .

(Ad Fam., XVI, 4, 1–3)

*November 13 came, and Curio's veto had still prevented a successor to Caesar being appointed. Curio's tribuneship ended, but on December 10 Caesar had Mark Antony ready to step into his shoes. By preventing the Senate from duly appointing governors, the tribunician veto was now making nonsense of the constitution.*

*Caesar now came south across the Alps.*

*On December 1 Curio once more moved the proposal, always suspect to Pompey, that Caesar and Pompey should lay down their commands simultaneously. It was passed by 370 votes to 22, but vetoed. Next day Pompey accepted command of the Republic's forces in Italy; it may have been news of this that made Hirtius think further negotiation futile, as related in the following letter.*

*To Atticus*            *Pompeii, December 10, 50 B.C.*

Dionysius was desperately anxious to be with you, so I let him go, with some regrets, I confess, but I had to consent. I knew already that he was well-educated, but I now find that he is also most loyal, solicitous for my reputation, honest and (not to give him merely a freedman's 'character'), a thorough gentleman.

I saw Pompey on December 10; we were perhaps two hours together. He seemed to be delighted at my arrival, encouraging about my Triumph and ready to play his part; but he warned me not to enter the Senate before I had finished the job, for fear of offending some tribune by the sentiments I expressed there. In short, so far as words help, he couldn't have been more profusely helpful.

As for the political situation, he spoke as though war was a certainty, and held out no hopes of agreement. He said that he had long believed that Caesar was estranged from him, but now he knew it for certain: Hirtius, one of Caesar's most intimate friends, had been in Rome and had not come to see him. Hirtius had arrived on the evening of December 6, and Balbus had arranged a meeting on the whole situation between him and Pompey's father-in-law, Scipio, for before daybreak next day, but late that night Hirtius went off to join Caesar again. This seemed to Pompey to be proof positive of estrangement.

So then I have no consolation except the thought that, when even Caesar's own enemies have given him a second consulship and fortune has given him the mastery, he cannot be so mad as to jeopardise these advantages. But if he runs amok, many's the fear I have, and I dare not commit them to writing. As things are, however, I'm thinking of coming to town on January 3.                                      (*Ad Att.*, VII, 4)

*To Atticus, at Rome*                              *Formia, December* 18, 50 B.C.

... You say that there is wonderful interest in my arrival, and that no good, or even moderate, patriot is in any doubt what I am going to do. But I don't know who you mean by 'patriots'. If you mean a class, I don't recognise them; there are only individual patriots; but when it comes to a split, it is the patriotic *class* or *party* we must find. Do you think the Senate is patriotic, leaving our provinces without governors? (Curio could never have held out, if negotiations had been begun with him: but the Senate turned that down, so no successor to Caesar was appointed.) Or is it the tax-farmers, never a reliable class and now hand in glove with Caesar? Or the financiers? Or the farmers, whose motto is 'Peace at any price'? Do you think they will be afraid of having a despot, when they never have objected to having one so long as they were left in peace? What then? Do I approve of a man being allowed to stand for the consulship who has retained his army beyond the prescribed date? No, not even of his standing in his absence; but when the one privilege was granted, it implied the other. Did I approve of his being granted ten years of military command, and of the way the measure was carried? If I did, I should have to approve of my own banishment, the squandering of the Campanian allotments, the adoption of a patrician by a plebeian and of a citizen of Cadiz by a citizen of Mitylene, the fortunes amassed by Labienus and Mamurra, and the gardens and Tusculan estate of Balbus.

But the source of all these evils is one and the same: we ought to have resisted him while he was still weak—and it would have been easy; now he has eleven legions, all the cavalry he wants, the peoples north of the Po, the city mob, and all these Tribunes of the People and young men gone to the bad—himself a leader of supreme prestige and daring. Either we must fight him, or we must let him stand in accordance with the law. 'Fight', you say, 'rather than be slaves.' What's the use? If you lose, you'll be outlawed; if you win, you'll still be slaves. 'What will you do then?' Why, what livestock do: when scattered, make for your own sort. As the cow joins the cattle-herd, I shall join the patriots, or so-called patriots, even if they stampede to destruction. I see clearly what is the right course in these damnable straits. No one can tell what will happen when the fighting breaks out; but anyone can tell that, if the patriots lose, Caesar will be no more merciful than Cinna was in killing off the nobility, nor more restrained than Sulla was in plundering the well-to-do.

I've gone on for a long time to you about politics, and would go on longer, only my lamp is going out. Here, then, is the conclusion: 'Marcus Tullius, speak.'[1] 'My vote is for Pompey,—that is, for Pomponius Atticus.'

Please remember me to Alexis, a very nice boy—or has he become a man since I was away? He seemed to be getting on that way.

(*Ad Att.*, VII, 7, 5–7)

---

1. Thus the presiding officer would ask for his vote in the Senate.

# IV

# January to June 49 B.C.

*At the beginning of January, 49, while Cicero was approaching Rome,
Pompey's father-in-law, Scipio, proposed in the Senate that Caesar should
be ordered to lay down his command by a date to be fixed, on pain of being
declared a public enemy. The new Caesarian tribunes, Mark Antony and
Quintus Cassius, tried to use their veto, but were expelled. They left
Rome with Curio and Caelius and reached Rimini on the 10th. Caesar was
near Ravenna, and on the night of the 11th he crossed the Rubicon, the
little river north of Rimini that divided his province of Hither Gaul (the
Po Valley) from Italy proper. The Civil War had begun.*

*To Tiro, at Patras*                    *Near Rome, January 12, 49 B.C.*
    . . . I arrived outside Rome on January 4. Nothing could have been
a greater compliment than the way people came out to meet me. But
I found the city inflamed with discord, or rather with civil war, and
when I wanted to heal the wounds, as I think I could have done, I
came up against the ambitions of particular individuals; for on both
sides there are people who actually want to fight.

The situation is, that Caesar himself, our old friend, has sent a bitter
and threatening letter to the Senate, and is still so insolent as to retain
his army and province against its will, backed up by my friend Curio.
Mark Antony and Quintus Cassius, expelled from the House, but
expelled without violence, went off with Curio to join Caesar after
the Senate called upon consuls, praetors, tribunes and us ex-consuls
to deal with a proclaimed state of national emergency.

Never has the State been in such danger; never have disaffected
persons had so well-prepared a leader. On the whole, however, our

side too are making great efforts to prepare. This is due to the influence and energy of our Pompey, who is beginning, now it is too late, to be afraid of Caesar.

In spite of these upheavals a crowded House demanded a triumph for me; but the consul Lentulus, to put me under a greater obligation to himself, said he would make a motion about this as soon as the measures demanded by the political situation had been taken. I am doing nothing in a selfish spirit and this increases the value of my prestige. Italy has been divided into regions with one man to be responsible for the defence of each. I have taken on Capua.

That's all I have to tell you. Be sure you take great care of your health, and write to me as often as you have anyone coming here. Do take care of yourself.                    (*Ad Fam.*, XVI, 11, 2–3)

*Cicero, while remaining ostensibly, and also in the last resort, a Pompeian, sought first of all to avert a clash and play the part of mediator, though this policy exposed him to the charge of sitting on the fence. While not following Caelius' principle of backing what looked like the winner, he was appalled at the outset by Pompey's prompt evacuation of the capital, and later by the incompetence and defeatism of the Pompeians in general. Caesar meanwhile, and his supporters who were friends of Cicero, Trebatius, Balbus, Oppius, Dolabella, Caelius, even Antony, did all they could to detach him from Pompey; they hoped that, if he would not give them the support of his prestige or his presence in Rome, at least they could get him to remain in Italy as a neutral. Any Pompeian caught by Caesar was set free, and this clemency by and large produced the desired effect.*

*To Tiro, at Patras*          Capua, near Naples, January 27, 49 B.C.
The extent of the danger to my own safety, and to that of all loyalists, and indeed of the whole Senate and State, you may gather from the fact that we have abandoned our homes and our city itself to be plundered and burnt. Things have become so bad that only luck or a miracle can save us.

Ever since I reached the area of Rome I have not ceased my efforts to further agreement by thought, word and deed, but an amazing passion has seized not only the ill-disposed, but also those who are reputed to be well-disposed: they are longing to fight, in spite of my protestations that nothing can bring more misery than civil war. So while Caesar, in a fit of madness, forgetting his honour and position, was sweeping through Rimini, Pesaro, Ancona and Arezzo, we abandoned the capital. It's no good arguing the wisdom or courage of this step now.

So you see our position. The upshot is, that he has sent the following terms: Pompey to go to Spain; our units already enrolled and our garrisons to be disbanded; he to hand over Further Gaul to Domitius, Hither Gaul to Considius Nonianus (the men to whom the provinces have been allotted); himself to come and canvas for the consulship, abandoning his claim to stand in absence, and to canvass in person for the regular twenty-four days. We are accepting the terms, on condition however that he withdraws his garrisons from the places he has occupied, so that the Senate may meet at Rome to discuss these same terms without being under a threat. If he does this, there is hope of peace—not peace with honour, for terms are imposed, but anything is better than our present state. If, on the other hand, he is unwilling to stand by his own conditions, all is set for a war; but it would be a war that he could not keep up, especially as he would have alienated people by defaulting from his own conditions, provided only that we cut him off from any chance of approaching the capital. This we hope could be done, as we are raising forces on a large scale; and we think he is afraid that, if he begins to make for the capital, he may lose the provinces of Gaul, both of which, except for the people north of the Po, are bitterly hostile to him; while in the Spanish theatre we have six legions and a large force of auxiliaries under Afranius and Petreius on his lines of communication. It looks as though, if he persists in his madness, he can be crushed, if only we keep Rome meanwhile. He has, besides, received a great blow in that the man with the greatest influence in his army, Titus Labienus, has refused to be a party to his crime: he has abandoned him and is with us, and many are said to be going to do the same.

Up to now I am regional commissioner of the coastal area southwards from Formia. I refused any more important post, so that my letters and pleas for peace might carry greater weight with Caesar. If, however, it is to be war, I see that I shall have to take command of a camp and regular legions. One of my troubles is that my son-in-law Dolabella is with Caesar. . . .            (*Ad Fam.*, XVI, 12, 1–5)

*To Atticus, at Rome*                     *Formia, February 2, 49 B.C.*

   . . . Trebatius writes to say that Caesar asked him on January 22 to write and beg me to stay near Rome: nothing I could do would oblige him more. All this at great length. I calculated from the date that as soon as Caesar heard of my departure, he had begun to worry in case none of us should be there. So I feel sure he has written to Piso, and to Servius too. What does surprise me is that he did not write to me himself, or do it through Dolabella or Caelius; not that I despise a letter from Trebatius, whom I know to be particularly devoted to me.

   I wrote back to Trebatius—not wishing to write to Caesar himself seeing that he had not written anything to me—saying how difficult it was to be there at this juncture, but that I was staying on my own estate, and had raised no forces nor undertaken any such commitment. I shall stick to this course so long as there is any hope of peace; but if it comes to open war, I will act as my honour and position require, after evacuating the boys to Greece; for in that case I can see the whole of Italy will flare up. This great disaster is the work partly of disaffected and partly of jealous elements. But how far things will go should emerge in a few days' time from his answer to my letter. I will write again then, if it is to be war; but if peace or even a respite, I shall hope to see you in person. . . .             (*Ad Att.*, VII, 17, 3–4)

*To Atticus, at Rome*       *Capua, near Naples, February 5, 49 B.C.*

   I must be short, as time itself is now short. I have lost hope of peace, yet the war effort on our side is non-existent. Make no mistake, nothing matters less to these consuls, on whose account, in the hope of hearing something and finding out about our preparations, I came to Capua, as instructed, on the 4th, in torrents of rain. They had not yet arrived, but were coming on the 5th, without equipment, without preparations. It was said that Pompey was at Lucera, and that units of Appius' not very reliable legions were approaching; but Caesar is reported to be tearing down and to be practically here, not to join battle (where's the opposition?) but to prevent escape. If the clash comes in Italy, well, *to every man upon this earth*—: on that I don't need your advice. But if abroad, what am I to do? Motives for staying are, the time of year, my bodyguard, and the improvidence and negligence of our leaders; for going, my friendship with Pompey, one's duty towards loyal citizens, and the disgrace of consorting with a despot—and we don't even know yet whether he will be a Phalaris or a Pisistratus.[1]

I wish you would unravel this knot and give me the benefit of your advice, though I realise you must now be having a feverish time yourself at home. But do what you can all the same. If I hear anything fresh here today, I'll let you know; the consuls will soon be here, being due on the 5th. I shall be expecting a letter a day from you. But answer this one as soon as you can. I have left Terentia and Tullia with the boys at Formia.                                (*Ad Att.*, VII, 20)

*To Pompey, at Lucera*                    *Formia, February* 16, 49 B.C.
    Marcus Cicero, Imperator, to Gnaeus Pompey, Proconsul.
    I received your letter at Formia on February 15, and gathered from it that things had gone much more satisfactorily in the Adriatic area than we had previously heard. I was glad to hear of Vibullius' courage and energy.

    So far I have stayed in the coastal area put under my command, but not without keeping a ship ready; for the news I had and my anxiety made me feel I should follow any course you enjoined. But now that your influence and directive have given me more grounds for hope, if you think Terracina and the coastal strip can be held, I will stay there. There are, however, no garrisons in the towns, as we have no member of the Senate in the district except Marcus Eppius, an alert and energetic man whom I have decided to leave at Minturnae; Lucius Torquatus, who is a strong man with influence, is not with me here at Formia, having left, I believe, to join you. . . .

    At present I do not know your intentions or the plan of campaign. If you think this coastal area should be held (and, besides having natural advantages and importance as well as excellent people in it, in my opinion it can be held) it must have someone in command. But if concentration is the plan, I feel no hesitation about joining you; nothing would give me more pleasure, as I told you the day we left Rome. If anyone says I have shown too little energy hitherto, I do not care so long as you do not think so; and in any case, if it comes to war, as seems likely, I am confident that I shall justify myself in everyone's eyes.

    1. Typical of malevolent and benevolent despots respectively.

I am sending you my relative Marcus Tullius, so that he can bring back any letter you care to send me.    (*Ad Att.*, VIII, 11B, 1; 3–4)

*To Atticus, at Rome*                    *Formia, February 16, 49 B.C.*

After I sent off my last letter to you a reply came from Pompey. The main part of it was about events in the Adriatic area as reported by Vibullius, and about Domitius' levy. You know about that already but this letter does not paint things in such glowing colours as Philotimus' did. I would send you the letter itself, but my brother's man is just leaving, so I'll send it tomorrow. But Pompey added a postscript in his own hand: 'I think you should come to Lucera. You won't be safer anywhere else.' This I took to mean that he counts the towns here and the coastal strip as a total loss, and it did not surprise me that the man who abandoned the head itself should have no compunction about the limbs. I replied at once by the hand of a trusted member of my staff that I was not looking for where I should be safest. If he wanted me for his own sake or in the public interest to come to Lucera, I would come at once. But I begged him, if he was looking to our overseas possessions for corn supply, not to give up the coastal area.

I realised that I was writing in vain, but I wanted to put on record now my opinion against the abandoning of Italy, as I did before in favour of holding Rome. For I see what is in the wind: to concentrate all our forces on Lucera, and even that not as a permanent stronghold but as a base for evacuation if we are hard pressed.

So you need not wonder that it is with little enthusiasm that I join a side which has never tried to plan for peace or victory, but always for disgraceful and disastrous retreat. I must go, because I prefer to endure with reputed loyalists whatever fate may bring rather than seem to disagree with any loyalists. Not but what I can see that very soon Rome will be full of loyalists, that is with rich and prosperous gentlemen—overflowing with them, when these provincial towns have been abandoned; and I should be with them, if I hadn't got this damned bodyguard.[1] I should not be ashamed to be seen with Manius Lepidus or Lucius Volcacius or Servius Sulpicius, not one of whom is a bigger fool than Lucius Domitius, or a worse trimmer than Appius Claudius.[2]

1. He could not dismiss his bodyguard of 'lictors' without forfeiting his chance of a Triumph.
2. These two were still with Pompey.

Pompey alone makes me hesitate, for his old kindness to me, not for his prestige: what prestige could he have in this cause, seeing that when we were all afraid of Caesar he was himself devoted to him, and now that he has begun to fear him he expects everyone else to be against him? Still, I shall go to Lucera, and perhaps he won't be pleased to see me, as I shall not be able to conceal my disapproval of what has been done up to now.

If I could get to sleep, I would not pester you with such long letters. If you have the same excuse, you may of course pay me back in my own coin.                                                              (*Ad Att.*, VIII, 1)

*To Atticus, at Rome*                              *Calvi, February* 18, 49 B.C.

In the throes of this terrible and wretched crisis I should like the benefit of your advice, even though we cannot discuss things together face to face. The whole question is this: if Pompey leaves Italy, as I suspect he will, what do you think I should do? To help you in advising me, I will briefly set out the points that occur to me on either side.

Not only a sense of Pompey's great services in the matter of my recall from exile and my intimacy with him, but also patriotism itself leads me to think that my policy should be linked with his, my fortunes with his fortunes. And another thing: if I stay in Italy and desert the company of all those true and eminent patriots, I must fall into the power of one man; and although he gives many tokens of being my friend (and you are well aware how I took steps long ago that he should be so, because I suspected this storm was blowing up), still there are two things to consider: first, to what extent can I trust him? and secondly, even if it is proved up to the hilt that he will be my friend, is it worthy of a brave man and a loyal citizen to remain in Rome, where once he enjoyed the highest rank and distinctions, performed great services and received high religious preferment,[1] but where he will now no longer be what he was, and will moreover be in danger, and to some extent also disgrace, if ever Pompey restores the constitution?

So much for the arguments on that side; now look at those on the other. Our leader Pompey has done nothing either wise or courageous, and, I may add, nothing that was not against my advice and authority.

    1. Cicero had been elected an augur in 53.

I leave aside those old scores; that it was he who nursed Caesar's career, built him up and armed him, he who aided and abetted him in passing laws by force when the omens were unfavourable, added Gaul beyond the Alps to his province, and married his daughter; he who officiated as augur at the adoption of Clodius into the Plebs, and showed less anxiety originally to prevent my banishment than later to get me recalled; he who prolonged Caesar's governorship and championed his cause in everything during his absence; he again who in his third consulship, after he began to appear as the defender of the constitution, still urged the ten tribunes to propose that Caesar be allowed to stand for the consulship *in absentia*, which privilege he confirmed by a law of his own, and opposed the consul Marcus Marcellus when he was for fixing March 1 as the closing date for Caesar's governorship of Hither and Further Gaul. Leave all that aside, and still—what could be more squalid and panic-stricken than this withdrawal, or rather disgraceful flight, from Rome? Any terms should have been accepted rather than abandon the Metropolis. The terms were unpalatable, I admit, but could anything be worse than this? You may say, Pompey will restore the constitution. But when? And what steps have been taken to that end? Haven't we lost the area round Ancona? Isn't the road to Rome wide open? Haven't we abandoned all our funds, public and private, to our opponents? In fact we have no policy, no forces and no rallying point for those who want the constitution defended. Apulia[1] has been chosen, the least populous district of Italy and the most remote from the brunt of this war; clearly despair commended it, as having a coast convenient for an evacuation.

I took on Capua with reluctance, due not to wanting to shirk the job, but to the nature of the cause; neither classes nor individuals had expressed any sympathy with it, except for a certain amount among the constitutionalists, who have shown their usual inertia. My own feeling was that the masses and the worst elements were on the other side, many of them simply out for revolution. I told Pompey himself I could do nothing without a garrison and without funds. So I have had nothing to do at all, since I saw from the outset that he was bent solely on flight.

But suppose I now think of escaping myself, where can I go? Not

1. Near the heel of Italy.

with Pompey: after starting out to join him I heard that Caesar was in the area, so that I could not rely on getting through to Lucera. I should have to embark from the west coast in the depth of winter and with no clear destination. Then again, with my brother, or with only my son? And in any case how? Either course would involve immense difficulties and immense heart-burning. And what revenge Caesar would take on me and my property while I was away! More severe than on others, since perhaps he may think he can do something to please the masses by doing me harm. Again these fetters, my fasces[1] and these lictors—what a business it would be to take them out of Italy! And what place will be safe for me, even supposing the sea calms down for the voyage, until I reach Pompey? I have no idea how or where to go.

But if I stand my ground, and find a niche on Caesar's side . . . my fasces are still a nuisance. Suppose he is well-disposed, which he may not be, but suppose it. He will offer me a Triumph. To refuse would surely be dangerous, to accept invidious vis-à-vis the loyalists. What a tough, insoluble problem! Yet solved it must be, for what other alternative is there?

I have said most in favour of remaining, but don't think that therefore I am particularly inclined that way: it often happens in a discussion that there is more talk on one side but more truth on the other. So in giving your advice please think of me as being open-minded on this all-important question. I have a ship ready both off my villa at Gaeta and at Brindisi. . . .                                    (*Ad Att.*, VIII, 3, 1–6)

*To Atticus, at Rome*                        *Formia, February* 25, 49 B.C.
On the evening of the 24th the younger Balbus came to me. He was hurrying on a secret mission to Lentulus the consul from Caesar, bearing a letter, messages and the promise of a governorship if he returned to Rome. I don't think he can be won over with a personal interview. He also said that Caesar wanted nothing better than to catch up Pompey (that I can believe) and be reconciled to him (that I cannot believe, and I am afraid all this generosity is only the prelude to another Reign of Terror). The elder Balbus writes to me that Caesar

1. The axes bound in rods which were the symbol of authority carried by the bodyguard of 'lictors'.

wants nothing better than to live in security under Pompey. I can see you believing that!

But even as I write this on February 25, Pompey may have reached Brindisi: he left Lucera on the 19th without baggage and ahead of his troops. But this instrument of wrath is terrifying in his vigilance, swiftness and energy. God knows what will happen.

*(Ad Att.,* VIII, 9, 1, 2)

*To Atticus, at Rome*            *Formia, March* 1, 49 B.C.

My secretary's handwriting will suffice as evidence that my eyes are bad and also as excuse for a short letter. Not that I have anything to tell you at the moment: we are simply waiting for news from Brindisi. If Caesar has caught up Pompey, there is a slender hope of peace, but if Pompey has crossed the Straits before that, I fear there will be a disastrous war.

Do you see what a man the Republic is up against, his foresight, his alertness, his readiness? I bet, if he kills no one and takes away nothing from anyone, he will be most adored by those who formerly were most afraid of him. The townspeople round here and the farmers talk to me a lot; they are interested in absolutely nothing beyond their acres, their homes and their savings. And observe how things have changed: they fear the man they used to trust, and love the man they used to dread. It hurts me to reflect what faults and weaknesses on our side have led to this. But I wrote before to tell you what I thought was coming to us, and I am awaiting your reply.     *(Ad Att.,* VIII, 13)

*To Atticus, at Rome*          *Formia, March* 11, 49 B.C.

Still no news from Brindisi. Balbus has written from Rome that he thinks Lentulus the consul has crossed by now, and that his nephew did not manage to get the interview, since the latter got the news at Canosa and wrote to him from there. He adds that the six battalions which were at Alba had joined Curius via the Minucian Way; this he heard by letter from Caesar, who said he would soon be near Rome.

So I shall follow your advice and not bury myself at Arpino at this juncture; previously I wanted to celebrate my son's coming-of-age[1] there, and contemplated leaving this as an excuse to Caesar, but perhaps this very thing would offend him ('Why not rather at Rome?'). All

1. i.e. give him his gown of manhood. He was now 16.

the same, if I must meet him, I had far rather it were here. Then I shall be clear about what follows—the whither, the how and the when. . . .

I had just finished writing the above when the following letter arrived from Capua: 'Pompey has crossed the sea with all the troops he had with him. The total is 30,000, with the consuls, two tribunes and the senators that were with him, all with their wives and children. He is said to have embarked on March 4.[1] From that day on the wind has been in the north. They say he disabled or burnt all the ships he did not use.' A letter on this subject reached Capua for Lucius Metellus the tribune from his mother-in-law, Clodia, who has herself crossed over.

Hitherto I have been anxious and distracted, as the situation certainly warranted, when I could not think out the solution; but now that Pompey and the consuls have left Italy I am not so much distracted as consumed with self-reproach:

> Steadfast no more, my heart runs wild with grief.

Believe me, I am beside myself at the disgrace I see I have brought upon myself. To think that I should not be, first of all with Pompey, whatever his policy, and secondly with the loyalists, however imprudently they have managed their cause! Especially as the very people for whose sake I was hesitant about committing myself, my wife and daughter and the boys, wanted me to follow that course, and thought the other discreditable and unworthy of me. As for my brother Quintus, he said that whatever I decided would be right for him and he would be perfectly content to fall in with it. . . .

(Ad Att., IX, 6, 1, 3–4)

*To Atticus, at Rome*                              *Formia, March 26, 49* B.C.

I have no news, but I am writing this so as not to miss a day. On March 27, they say, Caesar will stop at Sinuessa. He has sent me a letter dated March 26 in which he says he is looking to me for 'resources' (in his previous letter he called it 'support'). I had written a letter full

---

1. This report was premature by a fortnight: Pompey evacuated his army on March 17.

of praise for the moderation he showed at Popoli. Here is the text of his reply:

'You divine correctly, from your intimate knowledge of my character, that nothing is further from my nature than cruelty. And while I derive great satisfaction simply from having acted as I did, I am jubilant at your approval of it. Nor am I shaken by the fact that those I set free are said to have gone off to make war on me again. It suits me perfectly that I should be true to my character, and they to theirs.

I hope you will be near at hand when I am in Rome, so that I may, as usual, avail myself of your advice and resources on every occasion. I should like you to know how delighted I am with your son-in-law Dolabella, and I shall feel that I owe this to him: he is sure to arrange it, if I know his kindness and his feelings of goodwill towards me.'

*(Ad Att.,* IX, 16)


*To Atticus, at Rome*                          *Formia, March* 28, 49 B.C.

I followed your advice on both points: I spoke in such a way as to earn Caesar's respect rather than his gratitude, and I persisted in my resolve—no going to Rome. Where I was wrong was in thinking he would be amenable: I never saw anyone less so. My decision, he said, amounted to condemning him, and if I did not come, others would be more reluctant. I said their position was different. After much argument he said, 'Then come there and discuss peace.' 'On my own terms?' I asked. 'Who am I,' he answered, 'to dictate to you?' 'Then,' said I, 'I shall take the line that the Senate objects to your going to Spain or transferring forces to Greece; and I shall express deep sympathy for Pompey.' He interposed, 'I cannot have such things said.' 'So I imagined,' I replied, 'but I don't want to be there precisely because I must either say such things and many others which I could not leave unsaid if I were present, or not go at all.'

The upshot was that, as though seeking to leave the door open,[1] he asked me to think it over. I could hardly refuse, and so we parted. The result is that I don't think he's very pleased with me. But I was very pleased with myself, a feeling which I had long got out of the way of having. . . .

I almost forgot to tell you Caesar's horrid parting shot, that if he

1. Or, to break off the discussion.

could not follow my advice, he would take advice from where he could, and would go to any lengths. You will say, 'Well, you found the man to be as you had described him. Did you heave a sigh?' Yes, I did. 'Tell me more.' What more is there? He is going straight to his house at Pedum, and I to Arpino. . . .          (*Ad Att.*, IX, 18, 1, 3)


*To Atticus, at Rome*                              *Formia, March* 30, 49 B.C.

I am not worried by your news that my letter to Caesar has got into circulation. Indeed I myself gave it to plenty of people to copy. In view of what has happened and is likely to happen I wanted to put on record my views about peace. And in urging him of all people to keep it I thought my easiest chance of influencing him would be to say that my plea was such as should appeal to a man of his wisdom. In calling that wisdom 'admirable' I was not afraid of seeming to flatter, since I was pleading for my country's safety, in which cause I would gladly have thrown myself at his feet. In the words 'spare a moment' I was not referring to peace, but asking him to give a thought to myself and my obligations. As for my protestation that I had kept aloof from the war, though it is an obvious fact, I did put it in writing with the object of increasing the weight of my advice; and my approval of his case had the same object.

But what relevance has this now? I only wish it had done some good. Why, I should not object to my letter being read out at a public meeting, considering that Pompey himself exhibited in public that letter he wrote to Caesar containing the words 'in view of your splendid achievements' (more splendid than his own and Scipio's? Well, the occasion demanded he should say so), and considering that two men like you and Sextus Peducaeus are going out to the fifth milestone to meet him. Look where he's going at this very moment, and where he's coming from,[1] what he is doing, and what he is going to do. How much more rabidly, too, will he believe in his cause when he sees you and people like you not only coming in crowds but with smiles of congratulation on your faces? 'Any harm in that?' you ask. None at all in your case. But the fact remains that the means of distinguishing real from counterfeit goodwill are getting blurred. What

1. Going to Rome, illegally, with an army, and coming from besieging the Republicans at Brindisi.

decrees of the Senate we shall see!—But I have written more openly
than I had intended.

I hope to be at Arpino on the 31st, and then to tour my country
estates. I was afraid I was never going to see them again.

*(Ad Att.*, VIII, 9)


*To Atticus, at Rome*                              *Arpino, April* 1, 49 B.C.

I have celebrated my son's coming-of-age at Arpino rather than
anywhere else, Rome being barred, and that has pleased the people
here. Not but what I could see that both they and people I passed on
my journey here were gloomy and depressed, so bleak and grim is the
panorama of this immense disaster. Men are being called up and drafted
into winter quarters. Such things are troublesome in themselves, even
when they are done tactfully by decent people for a just war: think how
hateful they must be now, when they are done brutally by criminals
for an abominable civil war! And don't imagine that there is any bad
character in Italy who is not here. I saw them all together at Formia.
Good Lord, there was not one of them I thought human! I knew them
all individually, but I had never seen them in the mass before.

Let us go forward, then, to where we have resolved, and leave our
all behind: let us set out to join the man who will be more pleased at
our arrival than if we had been with him from the first. Then we had
great hopes, but now I at least have none; nor has anyone else left
Italy who did not count Caesar as his personal enemy. God knows
I'm not doing this for the Republic, which I regard as completely
finished, but in case anyone should think I was ungrateful to the man
who relieved me from the misery of exile he had himself inflicted on
me, and because I cannot endure the sight of what is happening, or at
any rate is sure to happen. . . .                    *(Ad Att.*, IX, 19, 1–2)


*To Cicero, at Formia, from Caelius*        *Near Marseilles, April* 16, 49 B.C.

Frightened to death by your letter, which showed you had some
project that could only be unfortunate, and without explaining fully
what it was betrayed the kind of thing you had in mind, I am writing
to you forthwith. If you care about your future, Cicero, and your
children, I beg and beseech you not to take any step that would
prejudice your welfare and safety. I protest before gods and men, and
in the name of our friendship, that I told you everything beforehand

and had good grounds for my warnings: as soon as I had talked to Caesar and ascertained what his attitude was likely to be when he had won, I passed on the information to you. If you think that Caesar will continue after that his policy of releasing his opponents and offering them terms, you are mistaken. His thoughts, and even his words, foreshadow nothing but cruelty and oppression. He left Rome in a rage with the Senate; he was obviously infuriated by the tribunes' using their veto; and believe me, there will be no place for appeals for mercy.

So if you have any regard for yourself, your only son, your home and your future happiness, and if you pay any attention to me and to your excellent son-in-law (and you should not wish to face us with the awkward alternative of being compelled either to hate and abandon the cause on whose victory our own welfare depends or to entertain undutiful hopes contrary to your welfare), do finally consider this: any odium arising from your original hesitation has already been incurred; it would be sheer idiocy now to go against the victor, whom you were careful not to injure when the issue was still in doubt, and to join, now that they are in flight, men whom you refused to join while they were putting up a stand. Beware of deciding too hastily which is the best cause through anxiety to be on the side of 'the best people'.

But if I cannot altogether convince you, at least wait until the result of our Spanish operations is known: I may inform you that when Caesar arrives the whole peninsula will be in our hands. What hope the Pompeians have if they lose Spain, I do not know; and what your idea is in joining a lost cause, upon my word I fail to see.

What you intimated to me, though not in so many words, had already come to Caesar's ears, and no sooner had he said 'Good morning' to me than he launched into what he had heard about you. I said I knew nothing about it, but begged him to send you the sort of letter most likely to induce you to stay in Italy. He is taking me with him to Spain; otherwise I should have hurried to see you, where-ever you were, before going near Rome, and personally extorted a promise from you and used all my powers to restrain you.

Think it over again and again, Cicero, before you completely ruin yourself and those you love; don't fall 'with intent aforethought' into a pit from which you can see there is no escape. But if you are influenced by what the nobles will say, or feel unable to bear the arrogance and swagger of certain persons, my advice is that you choose some town unaffected by the war, and live there until these issues are decided, as presently they will be. In that case I shall consider you have acted wisely, and at the same time you will avoid offending Caesar.

(*Ad Fam.*, VIII, 16)

*To Atticus, at Rome*          *Cuma, near Naples, May* 19, 49 B.C.
My dear Tullia had a baby, on May 19, a seven-months' boy. She had a good delivery, which is something to be thankful for; but as for the infant, it is a puny creature.

So far I have been kept here by an astonishing calm, which has been more of an obstacle than the watch kept over me. All that reassuring talk of Hortensius' was eyewash. We shall see. The wretch has been corrupted by his freedman Salvius. So in future I will not write to you what I intend to do, but only what I have done. Every professional eavesdropper seems to have his ears open for anything I say. But if you have news about Spain or anywhere else, please continue to write, without expecting a letter from me until I reach my wished-for destination (unless I send something while on the way). But even this I write on tenterhooks: everything has gone so slowly and stickily. The foundations were badly laid and the rest is of a piece.

I am now going to Formia: perhaps even there the Furies will pursue me. To judge from your talk with Balbus, my idea of going to Malta is not approved, so can you doubt that Caesar counts me as an enemy . . . ?                    (*Ad Att.*, X, 18, 1–2)

*To Terentia*                    *Formia, June* 7, 49 B.C.
All these worries and anxieties with which I made you miserable (this is to me the most vexing part of it) and darling Tullia too, who is more than life to me, I have now got rid of completely. I only discovered what was causing them the day after I left you. During the night I was violently sick, and at once felt so relieved that the cure seemed the work of some god. No doubt you will render thanks to him devoutly and duly, as you always do.

I have good hopes that this ship of ours will prove a splendid one. I am writing this just after going on board. Next I will write a large number of letters to our friends, earnestly begging them to take care of you and Tullia. I would be telling you both to be brave if I did not know you were braver than any man. However, I hope things are shaping in such a way that you will be quite all right where you are, while I shall at least be striking a blow for the Republic with those who feel as I do.

Above all, take care of your health. Use at your discretion those of our country houses which are furthest from the military areas. If the price of food goes up, you will be able to live easily on the farm at Arpino with the staff from our house in Rome.

Young Marcus is in fine form and sends you much love. Good-bye, a thousand times good-bye.                                      (*Ad Fam.*, XIV, 7)

# V

# June 49 to March 44 B.C.

*So Cicero followed Pompey nearly three months after he sailed. For two years now we possess very few letters. We know that he stayed for a time in Atticus' house at Butrinto and then joined Pompey's camp in the autumn. There he was not well received, and he found the extremist ideas of the nobles repellent.*

*In the Spring of 49 Caesar had hurried from Rome to Spain and in a forty-day campaign secured the surrender of five out of the seven legions of what was Pompey's best army. By August the Peninsula was his, and he returned to Rome for a period of reforming legislation. His one set-back was the destruction of two legions under Curio by King Juba in North Africa. Pompey meanwhile controlled the Eastern Mediterranean from Greece, and also the sea.*

*Early in 48 Caesar crossed to Greece, and eventually defeated Pompey in the great battle of Pharsalus in northern Greece on August 9. Pompey escaped and made his way to Egypt, where he was murdered on landing. Caesar, following with a small army, occupied Alexandria.*

*Cicero was not at Pharsalus: he had been left ill at Durazzo in Albania. After the battle he did not join the die-hards who continued the war, Cato, Scipio, Labienus and Pompey's sons, Gnaeus and Sextus. He returned to Italy at the end of October, and was grudgingly allowed by Antony to reside at Brindisi. (Caesar had resumed the title of Dictator originally secured for him by his deputy Lepidus while he was in Spain, and made Antony his second-in-command.)*

*To Atticus, at Rome*        *Brindisi, November 27, 48 B.C.*
    . . . I have never regretted leaving Pompey's camp. There was so

much cruelty there, so much contact with uncivilised peoples, that
plans had been sketched out for the outlawing not merely of individuals
but of whole classes. Things went so far that in the mind of everyone
there the property of all of you who stayed in Italy was to be the
reward of Pompey's victory. I say 'you' advisedly, for no one ever
thought of you personally but in the harshest way. So I shall never
regret my decision; it is the way I acted upon it that I regret. I wish
I had remained in some town over there until I was summoned back
to Italy: I should have caused less talk, suffered less distress and been
spared this feeling of self-reproach. To be hanging about at Brindisi
is trying from every point of view. How can I go nearer Rome, as you
advise, without the bodyguard given me by the people? To take them
from me would be to rob me of my rights. Even so, on approaching
Brindisi I made them for the time being mix with the crowd with
only single sticks in their hands, for fear of provoking assaults from
Caesarian troops. For the rest of the time I have stayed indoors.

I have written to Oppius and Balbus to give their minds to the
question how I should move nearer Rome. I think they will advise it.
They undertake that Caesar will be anxious not only to preserve but
to enhance my prestige, and encourage me to expect with every
confidence the fulfilment of my dearest hopes.[1] They promise and
guarantee this; but I should have felt more certain of it if I had stayed
in Italy before.

But I am harping on the past. Will you please consider the future
and go into the matter with those two; and if you think it necessary
and they approve, get hold of Trebonius and Pansa, and anyone else
suitable, to write to Caesar that whatever I have done had had their
sanction, since he is more likely to approve of the step I took if he
thinks it had the support of people on his side.

I am frightened to death by Tullia's illness and delicate physique.
But I know you are taking great care of her, and am most grateful.

I never had any doubt how Pompey would end. The faith of all the
kings and peoples in his success had been so shattered, that I thought
this would happen wherever he went. I cannot help being sorry about

1. Even now Cicero clung to his hopes of a Triumph, hence his anxiety to
retain his bodyguard, the symbol of the 'imperium' or command which a Triumph
presupposed.

his fate: in my experience he was an honest, clean and upright man. . . .

*(Ad Att.,* XI, 6, 2–5)

*To Atticus, at Rome*                                   *Brindisi, June* 19, 47 B.C.

There has been no rumour yet of Caesar's having left Alexandria: on the contrary, he is thought to be in a tight corner there. So I am not sending my son to him, as I had intended, and I implore you to get me away from here. Any punishment is better than lingering on like this. I have written about it to Antony, and also to Balbus and Oppius. Whether there is fighting in Italy or Caesar decides to use his fleet (one or other alternative must happen, and both may) this is the last place for me. I quite understand from your account of what Oppius said how angry the Caesarians are with me, but I am asking you to appease them. I no longer expect anything but unhappiness, but nothing could be more damnable than my present position. So please have a word with Antony and the rest and do the best you can for me, and write about everything as soon as possible.

*(Ad Att.,* XI, 18)

*Caesar had had other anxieties besides being besieged in Alexandria. Antony was having trouble in Italy. In 48 Caelius as praetor had raised a revolt aimed at debt-cancellation, which, however, cost him his life. In 47 Dolabella tried to do the same, but being potentially useful he was subsequently pardoned.*

*To Atticus, at Rome*                                   *Brindisi, July* 5, 47 B.C.

. . . I am worn out and worried to death by the difficulties of my poor, poor daughter. Was there ever such a state of affairs? If there is any way in which I can help her, I wish you would tell me. I can see you will have the same difficulty as before in advising me, but there is nothing that gives me more anxiety than this. I was blind to pay the second instalment of her dowry. I wish I hadn't; but that's all past history.

Do please, in view of the hopeless situation, raise any money you can from the sale of our plate and fairly plentiful furniture, and see it is collected and deposited in a safe place, since it seems to me that the crisis is coming now, there will be no negotiations for peace, and the present regime will collapse even without being attacked from outside.

You can discuss the matter with Terentia if you like, as occasion permits: I can't go into all the details.          (*Ad Att.*, XI, 25, 3)

*To Atticus, at Rome*                                    *Brindisi, July* 9, 47 B.C.
    . . . Do please give your mind to my poor girl's affairs, both about the matter I mentioned the other day, so that something may be done to keep her from destitution, and also about the will itself. One thing I wish I had done before, but I was afraid to do anything: the least of many evils was divorce. I should then have done at least one thing like a man, and I could have alleged either his advocacy of the cancellation of debts, or his nocturnal raids on houses, or his relations with Metella, or his general behaviour; I should have saved my money, and shown some manly indignation. I well remember your letter, but I remember also how things were at the time. Still, anything would have been better than this.
    Now it looks as if Dolabella were going to begin proceedings for divorce himself. I have heard about his statue of Clodius. To think that any son-in-law of mine should do that, or propose debt-cancellation! So I agree with you that we should serve notice on him. Perhaps he would then demand the third instalment of her dowry, so consider whether we should await his initiative or act first.[1]
    I will do all I can, even travel by night, in an attempt to see you. Please write about what I have mentioned above and anything else that may concern me.                              (*Ad Att.*, XI, 23, 3)

*To Atticus, at Rome*                                *Brindisi, August* 6, 47 B.C.
    . . . What follows will be in my own hand, as I have more confidential matters to discuss. Please take steps even now about Terentia's will, which was made at the time when she began to get into difficulties. I believe she did not bother you about it, as she never asked even me anything. But even so, since you have already touched on it in conversation, you will be able to advise her to entrust the will to someone who is not personally involved in this war. I should myself prefer it to be you, if she agreed. I am concealing from the poor woman what my fears are.[2]
    About the other matter, I realise that nothing can be put up for

    1. If Dolabella began proceedings, he forfeited all the dowry; if Tullia began them, then he retained at least part, unless she could prove misconduct.
    2. That her property would be confiscated.

sale now, but things could be stowed away and hidden so as to escape the impending crash. When you say that your resources and mine will be available for Tullia, I believe it of yours, but what resources can I have?

As to Terentia, apart from innumerable other instances, can you beat this? You wrote to her to send me a bill of exchange for twelve sestertia, saying that that was the balance of the money. She sent me ten, with a footnote saying that was the balance. If she keeps back so trifling a fraction of so small an amount, you can easily see what she has been making out of big transactions. . . .

(Ad Att., XI, 24, 2–3)

*To Terentia, at Rome*          *Venosa, October* 1, 47 B.C.

I expect to arrive home at Tusculum either on the 7th or the 8th. See that everything is ready there. There may be several others with me, and we shall, I think, be staying there for some time. If there is no basin in the bathroom, have one put there; and in general see that things are clean and there is enough to eat.      (*Ad Fam.*, XIV, 20)

*Long ago, in September,* 57, *we found Cicero apparently hinting to Atticus that Terentia was somehow at fault. By now he knew she had been cheating him systematically over money. We know besides that she had a disagreeable temper; and now, after thirty years of married life, he divorced her, even though the necessity of repaying her dowry would add to his financial embarrassments. Not long afterwards he married his ward, Publilia, a rich and very young girl.*

*Meanwhile Caesar, after protracted delays, had returned to Italy. Shortly after his landing at Taranto he met and pardoned Cicero, who was now free at last to return to Rome.*

*Unable to play any decisive part in politics, Cicero turned to writing, more to take his mind off the present than for its own sake. The result was momentous for Europe. In three years he produced the series of discourses and dialogues which, besides inventing for the Latin language a philosophic vocabulary, familiarised the Romans and ultimately all Western Europe with Greek ideas. They are works of philosophic journalism rather than philosphy, but they profoundly influenced both the early Church and the Renaissance Humanists; and only two centuries ago 'Tully's Ends' and 'Tully's Offices' (The* De Finibus *and the* De Officiis) *were among the staples of English education.*

E

*To Varro*[1]                                                    *Rome, early in* 46 B.C.

From your letter to Atticus, which he read me, I found out what you are doing and where you are; but it gave me no inkling when we were going to see you again. However I am beginning to hope that your arrival will not be long delayed. May it bring me the comfort I need! Our troubles are so great and so numerous that no one with a grain of sense should expect any relief from them; and yet there are ways in which you can help me, and I perhaps help you. For I must tell you that, since my return to Rome, I have re-established good relations with certain old friends, namely my books. Not that it was through any irritation that I had given up intercourse with them, but rather through a slight feeling of shyness; for it seemed to me that in plunging into a whirl of activity in most unreliable company I had paid too little attention to their advice. They forgive me, invite me back to our old intimacy, and say that you were wiser than I for never having broken with them.

And so, since I am on good terms with them again, I think I can reasonably hope that, if I see you, I shall easily weather both present and impending storms. So whether we meet at your house at Tusculum or Cuma, or (my last choice) at Rome, so long as we are together, I shall certainly make sure that we are both glad we met there.

(*Ad Fam.*, IX, I)

*In December,* 47, *Caesar had crossed over to Tunisia to deal with the Pompeian forces which had long been concentrating there in considerable strength. In April,* 46, *he utterly defeated them at Thapsus, and Cato committed suicide at Utica. The news had not yet reached Rome when the following letter was written.*

*To Atticus*                                                    *Rome, April,* 46 B.C.

Whatever you say, there are rumours here that Murcus has been lost at sea, that Pollio got ashore only to fall into the hands of Pompeian soldiers, that this adverse gale has made fifty ships put into Utica, and that young Gnaeus Pompey is nowhere to be seen and has not been to the Balearics at all, in spite of what Paciaecus maintains. But there is no authority for anything. I am just telling you what people have been saying while you've been away.

1. The most learned and encyclopaedic writer of the age.

Meanwhile there is a festival at Palestrina. Hirtius and all that lot are there. Eight whole days of celebration! What dinners, what frivolities! And perhaps meanwhile the great issue has been decided! They amaze me, these people. There's Balbus; he's building: *je m'en fiche* is his motto. But if you ask me, I think a man is finished when he makes pleasure, not duty, his main object.

Meanwhile you slumber on. But now is the time to solve the problem, if you are going to do any good. . . . I shall be seeing you soon, and hope you'll come straight to my house from your journey. We will fix up a day with Tyrannio when we meet, and anything else there is to do.                                   (*Ad Att.*, XII, 2)

*To Varro, at Tusculum*                     *Rome, late in April*, 46 B.C.

. . . I will give you the same advice as I give myself: let us avoid men's eyes, even if we cannot so easily avoid their tongues. For those who are pleased with themselves for having won look upon us as defeated enemies, while those who are distressed at our friends' defeat resent our being alive. Perhaps you will ask why, this being the state of affairs at Rome, I have not kept away from there, as you do. You, I suppose, being so much more far-sighted than I or anyone else, foresaw everything and made no false step at all; but who is so lynx-eyed as to stumble over nothing and run into nothing in darkness like this?

Long ago it occurred to me too that it would be very nice to go off somewhere else, to avoid seeing and hearing the things that are being done and said here. But I was over-sensitive: I thought that everyone I met, according to his inclination, would be suspicious, or even if not suspicious, would say: 'This fellow is either frightened and is running away for that reason; or he is hatching a plot and has a ship ready.' Even those who took the most lenient view and perhaps knew me best would think that my reason for going was my inability to bear the sight of certain persons. It is because of such misgivings that I still remain in Rome. Besides, daily experience has by now insensibly made me thick-skinned and deadened my indignation.

That is the explanation of my policy. As for you, my advice is as follows: lie low where you are so long as this feverish rejoicing lasts and until we know also how the whole affair has been settled, for settled I think it is. Much will depend on the temper of the victor, and on the sequel. I can make a shrewd guess, but all the same I'm waiting to hear.

I don't like the idea of your going to Baiae, unless these rumours will have grown hoarse with shouting. It will be more to our credit, even when we leave Rome, to be thought to have gone to those parts to indulge in mourning rather than in bathing. But you can judge better. Only let us keep our resolve, to live together in pursuit of our studies, to which we used to look for pleasure only, but now look for salvation also; and if anyone is willing to use us not only as architects but even as workmen to rebuild the Republic, not to refuse but gladly to lend a hand; and if no one avails himself of our services, at any rate to read and compose 'Republics', and if we cannot guide the State from the Senate-house and Forum, at least to guide it from the study and library, as the great thinkers of old used to do, and to investigate ethics and politics.

That is my view. I should be most obliged if you would write and tell me what you think and what you are going to do.

(*Ad Fam.*, IX, 2, 2–5)

*To Atticus, at Rome*          *Tusculum, near Rome, June* 14, 46 B.C.

How relieved I was to get your delightful letter! So I am to have my red-letter day after all! I had been anxious because Tiro said you looked rather flushed to him. I will stay on another day then, as you wish.

But about Cato, it would take an Archimedes to solve the problem. I cannot contrive to write an obituary your Caesarian cronies would read with tolerance, let alone satisfaction. Why, even if I steered clear of his speeches in the House and of all his political ideals and policy, and chose merely to give an unvarnished eulogy of his upright and single-minded character, even that would be a distasteful recital to them. Yet he is a man to whose merits one cannot do justice without elaborating the following points: he foresaw the events that are now happening; he laboured to prevent their happening; and he preferred to die rather than see them happening. What is there here that could win the approval of a man like Aledius?

Do take care of yourself, and apply first of all to getting well the good sense you apply to everything else.

(*Ad Att.*, XII, 4)

*To Paetus, at Naples        Tusculum, near Rome, early in July, 46 B.C.*

I was charmed with your letter, and, all else apart, much affected by your affection for me, which prompted you to write for fear Silius' message might have caused me some anxiety. You yourself had written to me about it before, twice in fact in the same terms, which clearly conveyed to me that you were perturbed,[1] and I had written you a careful reply designed as best I could in such circumstances to relieve your mind of this worry completely, or at least considerably.

But since your last letter too shows how worried you still are about it, let me tell you this, my dear Paetus: whatever strategy could do—ordinary planning for battle is no longer adequate: we must think out a stratagem—everything, then, that could be concocted or accomplished to win and secure the goodwill of those people has had my most serious attention; and not without success, I think; for I am treated with such respect and esteem by all who enjoy Caesar's favour that I do believe they like me. It is hard, of course, to distinguish real from assumed goodwill, unless some crisis occurs in which the sincerity of benevolence may be tested by danger, as gold is by fire; but while all the other signs could mean anything, I have one good reason for thinking that they really and truly do feel friendly to me, and that is that both my condition and theirs are such as to make pretence pointless. And from the man who holds all the reins of power I can see nothing for me to fear—except that everything is uncertain when once you get away from law, and there is no guarantee what will happen when all depends on another's will, not to say whim.

However, as for himself, I have done nothing to offend him. For in this very matter, I have behaved with extreme self-control, and while previously I thought that it was my business to speak freely, inasmuch as it was through my efforts that freedom still existed in the State, now that that has been lost, I think it my business to say nothing to alienate either him or those in his favour. If I wished to escape being credited with certain smart or witty sayings, I should have to sacrifice my reputation as a wit; and were this possible, I should not refuse. But Caesar himself has a penetrating sense of style, and just as

1. Paetus had apparently warned Cicero that people were repeating to Caesar indiscreet epigrams attributed to him, and quoted the tragedian Accius for the way that envy can undermine.

your brother Servius, a consummate literary critic in my opinion, could easily say, 'This line is not by Plautus, but that is,' because his ear was trained by noting the different styles of poets and by constant reading, so I am told that Caesar, having now filled whole albums with *bon-mots*, rejects anything not by me that is submitted to him as being mine. And this he does all the more now that friends of his are in almost daily contact with me. As our talk ranges, it often happens that I say things which strike them perhaps as being not without point or wit. These they repeat to him along with the news of the day (those are his own instructions). And the result is that if he hears anything else attributed to me, he dismisses it.

For this reason I have no use for your quotation from the *Oenomaus* of Accius: it was apposite, but where does envy come in, or what is there for anyone to envy me now? And even suppose there was everything: I observe that the only philosophers who seem to me really to know the meaning of virtue hold that a wise man can guarantee nothing but his own innocence: and I think I am doubly innocent, both because I perceived the ideal solution, and because, when I saw that the physical means of achieving it were lacking, I declined to struggle against superior force. So I am free from blame on the score of my duty as a loyal citizen. It only remains for me to do or say nothing foolish or rash against those in power; and that too seems to me to be the wise man's part.

As for the rest, what various people say I have said, or how he takes it, or how trustworthy as companions are these people who make a point of treating me with respect and esteem, I have no guarantee. Consequently I console myself with my good conscience as to my former intentions, and with my self-control at the present time, and I will apply your simile from Accius, not to envy, but to fortune's dart, which is to my mind a light and feeble thing that should 'recoil shattered' from a stout and constant heart 'like a wave from a rock'. And besides, if the records of Greece are full of examples of how the greatest sages behaved under tyranny at Athens or at Syracuse, when all around them their cities were in slavery but they themselves were somehow free, may I not hope that I can keep my status in the same way, so that I neither offend anyone nor lose my dignity?

Now I come to your jokes—since you put on after the *Oenomaus* of Accius not a comedy, as the custom used to be, but a farce, as they do nowadays. What's this you tell me about cat-fish and chips[1] and a nice bit of stock-fish *au gratin*? I used to be very polite and put up with that sort of thing: now things have changed. I have Hirtius and Dolabella as my pupils in the art of speaking and teachers in the art of dining. (I expect you have heard, since you people don't miss much, that they come regularly to me to declaim, and I go to them to dine.) It's no good your pleading insolvency to me: when you were making money, the effect was that you counted every penny; now that you are losing it so cheerfully, why not look at it like this?—entertaining me is no worse than getting a reduced valuation: even this blow comes better from a friend than a debtor.[2] However, I do not demand the sort of dinner from which a lot will be left over; but what there is must be grand and luxurious. I remember your account of Phamea's dinner: yours must begin earlier, but be otherwise just like that. But if you insist on getting me back to your old mother's kind of dinner, I will put up with that, too. For I should like to see the man who dared to put before me the things you mentioned, or even a polypus turned out as red as a painted statue of Jove.[3] Believe me, you will not dare. The rumour of my new luxuriousness will precede me, and you will be cowed. And it's no use your relying on the hors-d'œuvres; I've given them up entirely; your olives and sausages used to take the edge off my appetite.

But enough of this. I only hope I can get there. Please—my one desire being to put your fears to rest—go back to your old stock-fish *au gratin*. The only extra expense I shall cause you is that you'll have to heat the bath-water: the rest as usual: all that was just fun.

Thank you for your careful investigations and most amusing description of Selicius' house. In that case I think I'll let it go. More smart than solid.  (*Ad Fam.*, IX, 16)

*To Paetus, at Naples*      *Tusculum, near Rome, late in July*, 46 B.C.

I was having a holiday at my place at Tusculum, having sent off my pupils to meet their friend Caesar and incidentally to do their utmost to put me in his good graces, when your extremely charming letter arrived. I gathered you approved of my scheme of opening a kind of school,

1. The text is corrupt, but the context seems to demand some such reference.
2. Caesar had passed a law compelling creditors to accept land from debtors at pre-war valuation (a loss of 25 per cent).
3. At one time Jupiter's image was painted red for festal appearances.

now that courts of justice are a thing of the past and I am no longer King of the Forum, just as King Dionysius is said to have done at Corinth after he was driven out of Syracuse.

I am delighted with the scheme myself. It has many advantages. In the first place—and this is the most important thing at the moment—I secure protection against the present evils.[1] How much it's worth, I don't know; I can only see that so far no one has suggested anything better—unless, of course, it would have been better to die. 'What? In bed?' Admittedly, but fate ruled otherwise, as for the battlefield, I wasn't there. The others, Pompey, your friend Lentulus, Scipio, Afranius, all died miserably.—But Cato, you say, died gloriously. Well, it's open to me to do likewise whenever I choose; but my one object should be to see it is not a necessity for me as it was for him; and that's what I am doing. So much for the first advantage.

In the second place, I am improving, both in my health, which suffered while I was not exercising my lungs, and also in my oratorical powers, such as they were, which would have withered away if I had not gone back to this form of exercise.

Finally there is an advantage which you would probably put first: I have now demolished more peacocks than you have paltry pigeons. You may be revelling there in 'The Sources' of Haterius, while I revel here in Hirtius' sauces.[2] So come, if you're worth your salt, and learn from me the principles of what you want to know; though it's a case of 'Teach your grandmother——'

Since apparently you cannot line your pockets by selling your valuation-lands, you'll have to migrate back to Rome. Better to die of indigestion here than of starvation down there. I realise you have lost money, and hope the friends that keep you at Naples have done the same. You're done for, then, if you don't take steps. You can ride to Rome on the mule you say is the only thing you have left, now that you've eaten up your pack-horse.[3]

You can be second master and have a chair next to mine in the school, with prospects of a cushion later.                          (*Ad Fam.*, IX, 18)

1. Since his 'pupils', Hirtius and Dolabella, had influence with Caesar.
2. Haterius was a famous jurist. There is a pun on a word (jus) meaning both 'law' and 'sauce'.
3. i.e. frittered away the money he got from its sale.

*To Paetus, at Naples*                          *Rome, August, 46* B.C.

I was delighted to get your letter, for two reasons: it made me laugh myself, and it told me that you were able to laugh again. I did not mind at all being overwhelmed with your volley of rotten tomatoes,[1] like a knock-about comedian; but I do mind not having been able to come to those parts, as I had intended; I should have been more like a member of the family than a guest. And what a man! Very different from the one who used to give in after your hors-d'œuvres. I come to the entrée now with appetite unspoilt, and so the good work goes on right up to the roast. My old virtues you used to praise—'So easy to entertain', 'Such an unexacting guest'—are all gone. I have cast away all my cares about politics, all my worries about how I should vote in the House, all my getting up of briefs; and I have deserted to the camp of my enemy Epicurus, not to the prevailing extravagance but to the elegant table you keep—or rather, *kept* in the days when you had money to spend (not that you ever had more estates to your name!). So be prepared: you have to deal with a man who has a big appetite and has learnt his stuff; and you know how these late-learners go to extremes. You must forget about your homely compôtes and pasties. I am such a connoisseur these days that I often venture to entertain your friend Verrius and Camillus—what paragons of refinement and good taste! And see how bold I have become: I have even given a dinner for Hirtius, but without the peacock. There was nothing in that menu my cook could not reproduce except the hot sauce.

So this is how I live. In the morning I am at home to many who are loyal citizens but depressed, and also to our cheerful victors, who are treating me at least with every sign of respect and benevolence. When the stream of callers has subsided, I settle down to my books, either writing or reading. People also come to interview me as a man of learning, just because I am a little more learned than they are. After that I devote all my time to exercise. I have done mourning for my country, longer and more deeply than any mother mourns her only son.

Take care and keep well, or I shall devour your substance with you lying in bed. For I am determined not to let you off even if you are ill.                          (*Ad Fam.*, IX, 20)

1. Another untranslatable pun, on *mala*, meaning either 'abuse' or 'apples'.

*To Paetus, at Naples*                                    *Rome, Autumn,* 46 B.C.

I have just taken my place at table, and am dashing off the rough copy of this to you in my note-book. Where? At Volumnius Eutrapelus', and what's more, two friends of yours are next to me, Atticus on one side and Verrius on the other. Are you surprised that my slavery has become so lighthearted? What else am I to do? I ask you— you're taking a course with a philosopher. Should I be in agony? Should I torture myself? What good would it do? And how long would I have to keep it up? Live in your books, you say. What else do you suppose I am doing? Could I be alive at all if I wasn't living in my books? But even with them, though one does not get bored, one must have a break. And when I desert them, though I get little out of the dinner itself—whereas dinner was the only subject for study you proposed to your philosophy lecturer Dion—still I fail to see what better occupation I can have before I betake myself to bed.

To continue. Next to Eutrapelus at table is Cytheris.[1] What! *Our* Cicero,

> The pattern and the cynosure of every Grecian eye,

in *that* sort of company? I swear to you, I had no idea she would be there. However even Aristippus, the pupil of Socrates, did not blush when taxed with having Laïs as his mistress. 'She's not my mistress,' he said, 'I'm her master.' (It's better in the Greek: you can make your own version.) As a matter of fact I never took any interest in that sort of thing when I was young, nor do I now that I'm old. What I enjoy is good company, where I speak à propos whatever comes up, and turn grumbling into shouts of laughter. Do you do any better, the man who ragged the philosopher himself, saying, when he asked if anyone had any questions, that the question of dinner had been worrying you all day, when the old bore was expecting you to ask whether there was one universe or an infinite number? ...

So that's how life goes on. Every day something gets read or written. Then, so as not to neglect my friends, I dine out with them, not only keeping the letter of the austerity law, if there still is one, but keeping well within it. So there's no need for you to dread my arrival. You will find your guest far more bent on fun than on food.

                                                                   (*Ad Fam.,* IX, 26)

1. An actress, mistress of Volumnius, and later of Mark Antony.

*To Paetus, at Naples*                              *Rome, Autumn,* 46 B.C.

Aren't you an ass to be asking me what I think is going to happen
to those boroughs and estates in Campania when you have had our
friend Balbus staying with you? As if I should know anything he does
not know, or as if, when I do know anything, I did not get it from
him. On the contrary, I should be much obliged if *you* would give *me*
information what is going to happen to us; you have had a man at your
mercy from whom, drunk if not sober, you could extract it.

But I don't go into such matters, my dear Paetus, firstly because for
four years now I have been lucky to be alive at all, if one can speak
either of luck or life when one has outlived the Republic, and secondly
because I am inclined to think that I really know what is going to
happen. What will happen is whatever pleases the powers that be;
and power will always be with those who have the arms. We ought
therefore to be content with whatever we are allowed. Anyone who
cannot put up with this ought to have died.

It is true that estates round Veii and Capena are being surveyed,[1]
and that is not far from mine at Tusculum. But I'm not alarmed; I
enjoy things while I may, and pray that I always may. If things turn
out otherwise, still, having with my well-known heroism and
philosophy decided that life was the fairest thing there is, I cannot but
feel affection for the man to whose kindness I am indebted for it. For
all we know, he would like there to be a Republic such as both he
perhaps wishes and we ought all to desire, but has not the means to
bring it about, owing to the number of people with whom he is
entangled.

But I am running on too far: I forgot it was you I was writing to.
You may be sure, however, that not only I, who am not in his confidence, but even the master himself does not know what is going to
happen. We are slaves to him and he to circumstances; he cannot know
what circumstances will demand, nor we what he is meditating.

I did not answer your letter before, not because I am usually casual,
especially about correspondence, but because I had no authentic
information, and I did not want either to worry you by suggesting
uncertainty or to raise your hopes by suggesting certainty. But I will
add this, which is the absolute truth, that I have heard nothing in the

1. For allotment to Caesarian ex-servicemen. These places are a little north of
Rome. Tusculum is a little south of it. Paetus feared for his estates near Naples.

past few weeks about the danger you mentioned. But you as a philosopher ought to hope for the best, be prepared for the worst, and put up with whatever may come.                              (*Ad Fam.*, IX, 17)

*The Republicans (as we may now call the Pompeians) rallied once more after Thapsus, in Spain, where Labienus and Pompey's sons eventually collected thirteen legions. At the end of 46 Caesar had to go there himself, and on March 17, 45, he defeated them at the Battle of Munda. Only Sextus Pompey survived to carry on the struggle.*

*To Cassius, at Brindisi*                              Rome, early in 45 B.C.
This letter would have been longer if the bearer had not asked for it just before he started; it would have been longer, too, if I had had anything funny to tell you (to be serious is hardly safe any more). Can we still laugh, then? My God, it isn't easy! Nevertheless, it's the only distraction we have from our troubles. Where is our philosophy then? Why, yours is in the kitchen, mine only in the way: I am ashamed to be a slave, so I make a show of being busy over other things than politics, to avoid the reproach of Plato.[1]

No reliable news yet from Spain, in fact, no news at all. I am sorry for my sake, but glad for yours, that you are away from Rome.

But the messenger is pressing me. Good-bye then, and remember me kindly as you always have done since you were a boy.

                                                  (*Ad Fam.*, XV, 18)

*In February Cicero suffered another great blow in the death of Tullia.*

*To Cicero, from Servius Sulpicius*[2]                     Athens, March, 45 B.C.
When I was told of the death of your daughter Tullia, I was of course as grieved and upset as I was bound to be; I felt that it was my tragedy too, and if I had been there, I should have been at your side, and should have expressed my sympathy to you in person. All condolence is a wretched and painful business, because those who should give it, relations and friends, are themselves equally distressed, and

1. i.e. he is declaiming and teaching Hirtius and Dolabella oratory. Plato's dictum was 'Be free, and fear slavery worse than death' (*Republic* 387B).

2. One of the great Roman jurists, now Governor of Achaea, a province which comprised most of Greece.

can hardly make the attempt for grief, so that they themselves seem to need a comforter instead of being able to serve as comforter to others. For all that, I have decided to write to you briefly a few thoughts for this occasion which have occurred to me, not that I think they will be new to you, but in case your sorrow may have clouded your vision for the moment.

Why should your own private trouble affect you so much? Think how unkindly fate has already treated us, robbing us of things that should be as dear to men as their children—country, reputation, position, our whole career. Could the addition of this one drop add anything to our cup of woe? What mind schooled in such adversity should not be steeled by now to take everything less hardly?

Or can it be for her sake that you are mourning? How often must the idea have occurred to you, as it has to me, that in these times people have not had a bad fate who have been allowed painlessly to exchange life for death! For what great incentive to living could she have in such an age, what possession or prospect or solace? To have a married life with some distinguished young man? You were welcome, no doubt, in virtue of your position, to choose any son-in-law you liked from the youth of today, if you could find one to whom you would confidently entrust any child of yours! So that she might have children, and the joy of seeing their success? Children who would be able to maintain freely the inheritance their father left them, and to stand in due course for each office, with freedom of action in public life and in promoting the interests of their friends? There is not one of these promises that has not been snatched away before it was ful-filled. To lose one's child, you will say, is a calamity. I agree; but to have to endure all this may well be worse.

There is one thought I should like to put to you which has been a great consolation to me, in case it may also be able to bring you some comfort. On my return journey from Asia Minor, as I was sailing from Aegina towards Megara, I began to look at the lands round about. Behind me was Aegina, before me Megara, to the right the Piraeus, to the left Corinth. There was a time when these were most flourishing cities: now they lie there in dust and ruins. I began to think to myself, 'Why, fancy us insignificant humans taking it hard when one of us dies or is killed, whose life must in any case be short, seeing that in one place "the relics of so many cities lie exposed". Come, control yourself, Servius, and remember you were born a mortal.' I assure you, I felt considerably better for that thought. Do try, if you will, to fix your attention on the same idea. Lately, at one and the same time, many outstanding men perished, the Roman people suffered a crippling loss, and all our overseas possessions were shaken: are you then so distressed for the loss of the little life of one poor woman? If she had not died now, she would have had to die a few years later, since she was born mortal.

Then take your mind too off these things, and turn to thoughts worthy of your role: that she lived while life had anything to give her; that she lived as long as we were still a free people; that she saw you, her father, hold office as praetor, consul and augur; that she was married to young men of the foremost rank; that she experienced almost every happiness; and that when the Republic was falling, she departed this life. What possible quarrel could you or she have with fortune on that score?

Finally, do not forget that you are Cicero, the man who used to give others advice and counsel, and do not be like those bad doctors who, when others are ill, profess to be skilled practitioners, but who cannot cure themselves. Take to heart the advice you always give to others and keep a firm hold on it. There is no sorrow that the passage of time does not diminish and soften. It is unworthy of you to wait for this to happen, and not use your wisdom to anticipate it. If there is any consciousness even after death, you may be sure that she, with her love for you and her devotion to all her family, does not want you to do as you are doing. Think of your lost one; think of your other friends and acquaintances, who are saddened by your sorrow; think of your country, and give it the benefit of your help and counsel wherever it is needed.

And one word more. Since our fortunes have sunk so low that we must stoop even to such considerations as this—do not give anyone the chance to think that you are mourning not so much for your daughter as for the condition of the State and the victory of your opponents. I do not like to say anything more to you on this subject, for fear of seeming to lack confidence in your discretion; so I will end with just this one suggestion. We have often seen you bearing prosperity most finely, and winning great praise for it: let us see for once that you can bear adversity no less well, and that your burden weighs upon you no more heavily than it should, lest people think that of all the virtues there is one that you lack.

As for my own affairs, when I hear you are in a calmer frame of mind, I will let you know what is happening here, and all about the state of my province.                         (*Ad Fam.*, IV, 5)

*To Servius Sulpicius, in Greece*        *Ficulea, near Rome, April,* 45 B.C.

I do indeed wish you had been at my side, Servius, as you said, in my great distress. I can readily imagine how much you might have helped me with your consolation and your perfect sympathy, if you had been there, because even reading your letter made me a little calmer. For you not only wrote things which could lighten my sorrow, but in consoling me showed how sorry you were yourself. However, your son, Servius, by paying me all the attentions that were possible at that time, showed clearly both his devotion to me and his sense of the pleasure that such an attitude towards me would give you. There have been occasions when I have been able to enjoy his attentions more, but I have never been so grateful for them.

Not only what you say and the way you almost share my suffering, but your personal influence fortifies me. For I am ashamed that I should fail to bear my misfortune as you, with all your wisdom, think I should. But I am overwhelmed sometimes, and almost give in to my sorrow, at the thought that I am deprived of consolations which were available to the other men with whose cases I compare my own. For Quintus Fabius, who lost a son who had been consul, a man of distinction and great achievements, Aemilius Paullus, who lost two sons within a week, Sulpicius Gallus of your own family, and Marcus Cato,[1] who lost a son of outstanding gifts and character, lived at a time when their own position, which they had won in the State, could be a consolation in their grief, while I, who had lost all those dignities which you mentioned and which I had toiled incessantly to attain, had this one solace left me, and now it has been taken away. I had already no more friends' interests, nor public responsibilities, to distract my thoughts; I had no inclination to plead in the courts; I could not bear the sight of the Senate House; and I reckoned, with reason, that I had lost all the fruits of my labours and my good fortune. But when I reflected that you and certain others shared this fate, and when

1. This is the elder Cato, and all these are figures of the old free Republic.

I broke myself in and made myself bear it patiently, I found I had a refuge where I could be at peace, one in whose sweet society I could lay aside all my cares and troubles. But now that this blow has fallen upon me, even scars that seemed healed break out afresh. Before, when I came in depressed from public affairs, there was a welcome at home to cheer me up; but now I can find no escape from my house of mourning in politics, nor any good in them to comfort me. So I shun both home and Forum, since home can no longer console me for my grief at the condition of the State, nor politics for my grief at home.

Hence I am looking forward all the more to seeing you as soon as possible. No amount of philosophising can bring me the comfort that I shall get from renewing my intercourse and talks with you. I have good hopes, however, from what I hear, that you will soon be back again. I have many reasons for being eager to see you again as soon as possible, and especially the desire to compare notes as to how we should get through these times. It is all a matter of securing the goodwill of one man who is both prudent and generous and, as I think I can discern, not averse to me and most friendly to you. This being so, it is still a matter for earnest consideration what plan we should adopt, not for any action, but for living in retirement by his kind permission.

(*Ad Fam.*, IV, 6)

*To Atticus, at Rome*                    *Astura, near Anzio, March* 11, 45 B.C.
    In trying to escape from memories which make me eat out my heart, I am taking refuge in telling you something. Whatever you think of it, please forgive me.

    The fact is that I find that some of the authors who are now my constant study recommend the very project I have often discussed with you, and for which I hope to win your approval. I am referring to the shrine to Tullia, and I hope you will give it as much thought as you have affection for me. Now I have no doubts myself about the design (I like Cluatius'), nor about the project (my mind is made up), but I do sometimes have doubts about the site. So please consider.

    I mean to consecrate her memory to the highest degree possible in this highly enlightened age, with every kind of memorial derived from the whole artistic achievement of Greece and Rome. Perhaps this will only succeed in keeping my wound open; but I consider myself already bound by a kind of vow or promise, and I am more concerned about the long ages when I shall be no more than about the little remnant of my life, which in any case I find too long. I have tried everything, but cannot find peace of mind. When I was composing the essay I told you about before, I was only keeping my sorrow alive. Now I cannot stomach anything, and find nothing so tolerable as solitude. (Philippus did not disturb me as I had feared; after paying me a visit yesterday he went back immediately to Rome). . . .

(Ad Att., XII, 18, 1)

*To Atticus, at Rome*            *Astura, near Anzio, March* 14, 45 B.C.
This is certainly a lovely place, right on the sea and within sight of both Anzio and Circeii; but, in view of the many changes of ownership which may occur in the countless years to come, I must find a way of securing that the site remains consecrated ground so long as Rome is Rome. I don't need a large income now, and can be content with quite a little. Sometimes I think of buying some gardens across the Tiber instead, for precisely the reason that I can think of nowhere so much frequented; but which I should buy is a matter for when we meet, provided only that the shrine must be completed this summer. But I leave it to you to settle about the columns with Apella of Chios. . . .

(Ad Att., XII, 19, 1)

*To Atticus, at Rome*            *Astura, near Anzio, March* 16, 45 B.C.
About Terentia's dowry, please clear up the whole affair all the more urgently. It was a high-handed proceeding of hers to make over the debt to Balbus.[1] Settle it on any terms. It is discreditable that the matter should drag on.

'The Island' at Arpino would be perfect in itself for the deification, but I'm afraid its being out-of-the-way would mean less widespread honour. So I am inclining to the gardens; but I'll have a look at them when I get to Rome.

About Epicurus, you shall have your way[2]; but in future I shall

---

1. Cicero had to repay Terentia her dowry. She assigned it to Balbus in payment of a debt she owed him. As a powerful Caesarian, Balbus could exert pressure on Cicero to pay.

2. Atticus had apparently begged for some fellow-Epicurean the role of defending Epicurus' philosophy in the dialogue Cicero was writing *On Aims* (*De Finibus*).

change my practice about characters in my dialogues. You wouldn't believe how some people long for a place in them. So I'll stick to the ancients; then no one can be jealous. . . .          (*Ad Att.*, XII, 12)

*To Atticus, at Rome*          *Astura, near Anzio, March 28, 45* B.C.
. . . Publilia has written to me that her mother will bring Publilius to have a talk with me, and that she will come too, if I will allow her. She begs and entreats me at some length to let her, and to answer her letter. You see what a nuisance it is. I have written back that I am even more low now than when I told her before I wanted to be alone; so that I don't want her to come at present. I thought that if I didn't answer, she would turn up with her mother; now I don't think she will. It was clear enough that she wasn't responsible for the letter. But I want to avoid what I can foresee—their coming here at all; and the only way to avoid it is for me to take wing. I would rather not, but I must. Now I want you to discover how long I can stay here without being caught. But behave, as you say, with tact.

Please suggest to young Marcus, but only if you think it's not unreasonable, that he should keep the expenses of his travel and his residence at Athens[1] within the sum due for rent from my property in the Argiletum and on the Aventine Hill. He would have been well content with that if he had stayed in Rome and rented a house there, as he thought of doing. In making the suggestion please also arrange the details of how I should supply him with what he needs out of those rents. I'll guarantee that neither Bibulus nor Acidinus nor Messalla, who I hear will be at Athens, will have more to spend than he will get out of those rents. So please first see who the tenants are, and what their respective rents are; then make sure there is someone who will pay punctually; and finally find out how much will be enough for his journey and his outfit. There is certainly no need of a carriage and horses at Athens. For what he will need on the journey we have more than enough at home, as you yourself observe.

(*Ad Att.*, XII, 32, 2–3)

*To Julius Caesar, in Spain*     *Astura, near Anzio, late in March*, 45 B.C.
I wish particularly to recommend to you Precilius, whose father is a connection of yours, an intimate friend of mine and a very good man.

1. Athens was something like a University city.

I am not only exceedingly fond of the young man himself for his modest, courteous, lively character and his exceptional friendliness to me, but I know from experience and appreciate that his father has always had the warmest regard for me. Now then: this is the very man who has always laughed at me and scolded me most for not attaching myself to you, especially when I was invited to do so by you with every mark of honour.

But never could he move this heart to do it.

For I could hear our nobles shouting:

'Be valiant and win praise from men unborn.'
So spake he, and dark clouds of woe fell on him.

Nevertheless they still try to console me: even now they want a man already singed to go up in a blaze of glory, crying:

Nay, die not meanly and all unrenowned,
But do a deed posterity shall hear.

But as you see, I take less notice of them now. So I turn aside from Homer's sublimities to the true precepts of Euripides:

I hate advisers ill-advised themselves.

That is a line much praised by the elder Precilius, who says that a man can both 'look before and after' and at the same time

Ever excel and tower above the rest.

But to return; I should be extremely obliged if you would welcome this young man with your characteristic courtesy; and while I think you will be inclined to do something for him for his own and his father's sake, please do a little more on account of my recommendation.

I have written you a new style of letter to indicate that this is no ordinary recommendation.                    (*Ad Fam.*, XIII, 15)

*To Atticus, at Rome*                    c/o *Sicca, near Rome, May* 1, 45 B.C.

It never occurred to me until after I left you that, when a mausoleum is erected, the equivalent of any sum spent on it above the maximum allowed by the law has to be subscribed to public funds.[1] That would not worry me much were it not that somehow or other—perhaps unreasonably—I should not like it to be called anything but a shrine. This being so, I am afraid we can only achieve our purpose if we change the site.

Please consider what there is in this. For although I am less distracted and have almost recovered my balance, I do feel I want your advice. So I implore you again and again—more than you wish or allow me to implore you—to give your whole mind to the consideration of this problem.                                                    (*Ad Att.*, XII, 35)

*To Atticus, at Rome*                    *Astura, near Anzio, May* 3, 45 B.C.

I want it to be a shrine, and nothing can root this idea out of my mind. I am anxious to avoid any resemblance to a tomb, not so much to avoid paying the subscription as to come as near as possible to deification. This I could achieve if I built it at my own place, but, as I've often told you, I'm frightened about change of ownership. Wherever I build it in open country, I think I can ensure that posterity will respect it as consecrated. You must put up with my whims—I know they're foolish. I feel I can tell you things I have not the face to tell even myself. But if you approve of the idea, the site and the plan, please study the law and send it on to me. If you think of any way of getting round it, we will take advantage of it.

If you are answering Brutus' letter, reproach him, unless you think it's out of place, for not putting up at my house at Cuma for the reason he gave you. Thinking it over, I can't imagine anything ruder he could have done.

And finally, if you approve of going on as we began in the matter of the shrine, please stir up Cluatius and make him look sharp, since even

---

1. A law to limit extravagant expense on funerals and mausoleums. Cicero was afraid that, if he made it a shrine, he would seem to be trying to evade the law But he wanted it to be a shrine, and for some reason the gardens near Rome were unsuitable. Possibly there were mausoleums there already, so that it would be harder to assert its distinctive character.

if we change the site, I think we shall need his help and advice. See you perhaps out at the house tomorrow.                    (*Ad Att.*, XII, 36)

*To Atticus, near Rome*          *Astura, near Anzio, May 9, 45 B.C.*
  I can tell from the brochure Hirtius has sent me what will be the general lines of Caesar's invective against Cato in reply to my eulogy: Hirtius has put together all the faults of Cato, but praised me highly at the same time. So I've sent it on to Musca to give to your copyists: I want it to be circulated widely, so please give your men orders to that end. . . .                    (*Ad Att.*, XII, 40, 1)

*To Atticus, at Rome*          *Tusculum, near Rome, May 26, 45 B.C.*
  No doubt I shall have your opinion about the gardens tomorrow, as you are going to look at them today; and about Faberius, when he has arrived.

  As for the letter to Caesar, I solemnly declare—I can't do it. And it is not the shame that prevents me, though that should be the chief obstacle; for where is the shame in flattery compared with the shame of our being alive at all? But as I was saying, it is not the shame that prevents me—I wish it were, for then I should be the man I ought— but I can't think of anything to say. For in the case of those exhortations to Alexander the Great composed by learned and eloquent men, just look what data they had. Here was a young man fired with ambition for the truest glory and desirous of advice conducive to immortal renown, and they exhort him to follow honour. There is plenty to say about that. But what can I say?

  However, I had rough-hewn something from the hard material which looked the beginnings of a likeness. This has been criticised because there were some things in it, both past and present, which were just a little bit highly coloured. I am by no means sorry, for I should be sorry now if that version had reached its destination. You observe how even that pupil of Aristotle, with all his genius and all his self-control, no sooner assumed the title of king than he became haughty, cruel and uncontrolled. Then how do you think this deity of the procession, this lodger with Romulus,[1] will enjoy a restrained

  1. Caesar's statue had been carried with those of the gods in a procession, and placed in the temple of Romulus. Cicero commented to Atticus that he would rather see him lodge with Romulus than with Safety. (In the legend Romulus was assassinated.)

letter of mine? I would rather he regretted my not writing than disapproved of what I wrote; but after all, he can choose. . . .

(*Ad Att.*, XIII, 28, 1–3)

*To Atticus, at Rome*                *Tusculum, near Rome*, May 27, 45 B.C.

I have heard about the gardens both from your letter and from Chrysippus, the architect. In the house, the vulgarity of which I have known of old, I can find little or nothing changed. However, he praises the larger bathroom, and says the smaller might be made into a winter suite. So a covered walk would have to be added, and the cost of making it the size of mine here at Tusculum would be only half as much in that district. For the erection of the shrine I want, there could be no more suitable place than the wood, which I used to know well; though no one went there then, I hear it is now very much frequented. There is nothing I should like better. In this 'For God's sake humour me, indulge my whim'.

For the rest, if Faberius pays his debt to me, don't ask how high you may go: I want you to outbid Otho. If I know the fellow, he isn't likely to bid wildly. Besides, I hear he is so hard hit that I doubt if he will be a buyer. Otherwise, would he have taken it lying down? But what's the good of speculating? If you get the money out of Faberius, let us buy even at a high price. If not, we can't even pay a low price. In that case we must fall back on Clodia. I have more to hope for in that quarter, as her plot is much smaller, and Dolabella's debt seems so safe that I feel sure I could even raise ready cash for it. But enough about the gardens. Tomorrow I shall expect either you or a reason why not, presumably connected with Faberius. But come if you can. . . .

(*Ad Att.*, XIII, 29, 1–3)

*To Atticus, at Rome*                             *Arpino*, June 24, 45 B.C.

Your letter about my dear little Attica pierced me to the heart, but it also healed the wound; for in reassuring yourself in the same letter you gave me assurance too, and so took away the pain.

You have given my speech for Ligarius a splendid puff. Next time I write anything I shall entrust the advertising to you. As for what you say about Varro, you know that the speeches and so forth I wrote previously were of such a kind that he could not be worked in anywhere. But later, when I began these more academic compositions,

Varro had already announced his intention of dedicating to me a really great and important work. Two years have passed and the old tortoise, going hard all the time, has scarcely progressed an inch, while I was preparing to repay him 'full measure pressed down and running over' for what he sent, that is if I could (even the text adds 'if thou canst').

Now I have pledged my dialogue *On Aims*, of which I think pretty highly, to Brutus, as you wished, and you told me he was quite pleased to accept it. So I must transfer to Varro the *Academica*,[1] in which the present speakers, eminent in rank but not at all in scholarship, are made to talk with inappropriate subtlety. Besides, the views expressed are those of Antiochus, which Varro strongly approves of.[2] I'll make amends to Catulus and Lucullus elsewhere, but only if you agree; so please write and tell me. . . .

Let us give our whole minds to the business of Scapula's garden. The day is getting near. (*Ad Att.*, XIII, 12, 1–3)

*To Atticus, at Rome*                    *Arpino, June 26, 45 B.C.*

Under the influence of the letter you wrote me about Varro I have taken the whole of the *Academica* out of the hands of those most noble interlocutors and transferred it to our friend, rearranging it so that there will be four books instead of two. They are certainly finer than the first draft, though a good deal has been cut out. But I should very much like to hear how you discovered that he would like it. There is one thing, at any rate, I am longing to know, and that is who you understood to be the object of his jealousy. Was it Brutus, by any chance? That was the only conclusion, but I should very much like to know.

The books have turned out, unless an author's natural egotism deceives me, such that even the Greeks have produced nothing like them of that kind. You won't regret the loss incurred in having the first edition of the *Academica* copied out to no purpose, since this one is far finer, shorter and better.

I don't know where to turn now, I should like to do something for

1. A dialogue *On the Human Understanding*.
2. It was not a question of dedication, but of who should have the chief part in the dialogues. Antiochus was the head of the New Academy at Athens, the eclectic school of philosophy to which Cicero adhered. Lucullus and Catulus were the unphilosophic nobles who were to be displaced in favour of Varro.

Dolabella, as he is so eager, but I can't think what, and at the same time 'I fear the Trojans' reproach'; even if I do find a subject, I shall not be able to escape criticism.[1] So I must either lie fallow or think up something.

But why bother about such unimportant things? My dear Attica, how is she, please? I am very anxious about her. But I often chew over your letters again, and that calms me down. Still, I am waiting for a fresh one.                                   (*Ad Att.*, XIII, 13)

*To Varro*                          *Tusculum, near Rome, July* 11, 45 B.C.
(*with a copy of the* Academica)

Although to demand a presentation,[2] whatever hopes of it have been raised, is unusual even for the public, unless it is very excited, yet I am so much looking forward to receiving what you promised me that, without of course demanding, I am giving you a hint: I am sending you herewith a quartette of not too shy reminders. You well know the 'face' that younger Academy has. From its ranks, then, I have called them up and sent them to you; but I'm afraid they may demand, whereas my instructions to them were to ask. Anyhow, I have long been in a state of expectation, but have held back from writing you anything before I received something, so that I could repay like for like as far as possible; but since you were writing more slowly, which meant, as I divine, more carefully, I could not restrain myself any longer from testifying, by such a work as I could compose, to my sense of the bond between us created by our studies and our friendship.

I have therefore made up a conversation supposed to have taken place between us at my house at Cuma when Atticus was there too. I have given you the role of Antiochus, which I thought I knew you would approve, and taken that of Philo myself. No doubt you will be surprised on reading it to find us saying things we never said: but you know the dialogue convention.

Some day, my dear Varro, we shall have plenty of talks, if you agree, about our own affairs. Too late perhaps; but while for the past we may blame the ill-luck of the Republic, it is in our own hands to make use of the present. I only wish we could pursue our studies in a

1. From Pompeians ('the Trojans'), for flattering a notorious Caesarian.
2. Play on a word meaning a gift, and hence also a show presented by an individual to the public.

time of peace and under a government stable if not good. Though in that case there would be other considerations which would provide us with responsibilities and duties not without honour, while as it is, what reason for living have we except our studies? For my part I can hardly go on living with them, let alone without.

But we can go into this more often when we are together. I hope your change of residence and new purchase will turn out satisfactorily, and I approve of your policy in the matter. Take care of yourself.

( *Ad Fam.*, IX, 8)

*To Atticus, at Rome*          *Tusculum, near Rome, July* 20, 45 B.C.
How delighted I was to get your letter! The procession was certainly a bitter pill but it is pleasant enough to know everything, even about Cotta's proposal.[1] And how splendidly the crowd behaved, in not even applauding Victory because of her unpopular neighbour!

Brutus has called on me and strongly approves of my writing something addressed to Caesar. I had agreed, but this procession has put me off.

Did you really dare send Varro my book? I wonder what his verdict will be. But when will he finish reading it?

As to Attica, I agree. It is something that her mind should be comforted by the ritual and by the religious associations of the spectacle. . . .

(*Ad Att.*, XIII, 44, 1–2)

*To Atticus, at Rome*          *Pozzuoli, December* 21, 45 B.C.
What a blessing to speed so formidable a guest with no unpleasant memories! Caesar proved most affable. When he had arrived at Philippus' house on the evening of December 18th, it was so crowded with soldiers that the room where he himself was to dine could scarcely be kept clear; two thousand men there were. I was getting worried about what would happen next day, when Cassius Barba came to the rescue. He lent me a guard. The men camped in the open, and my house was protected. Caesar stayed at Philippus' until about noon on the 19th, and let no one in; doing accounts with Balbus, I think; then he went for a walk on the shore. After one o'clock he repaired to my bath. Then he heard about Mamurra; it had no visible

1. That Caesar should take the title of king (cf. Shakespeare *J. C.* I, ii). For the procession, see p. 149n. Caesar's statue was carried next to that of Victory.

effect. He made careful toilet and came to table. He was taking a course
of emetics, so he ate and drank fearlessly and with relish, expensively
of course and elaborately, and not only that, but

> With food well cooked and seasoned,
> With good talk too, and in a word, with pleasure.

Besides this, his *entourage* were entertained in three rooms on a generous
scale. His humbler freedmen and slaves lacked for nothing: the
superior ones I entertained in style.

Need I say more? I showed myself a man of good breeding. However, he wasn't a guest to whom you would say, 'Do please come
again on your way back.' Once is enough. Our talk kept off serious
topics and was largely about literature. In short, he was delighted and
enjoyed himself. He said he would be spending a day at Pozzuoli, and
another near Baiae.

There you have the story of a visit, or should I say, billeting, which
was distasteful to me, as I said, but did not prove embarrassing. I shall
stay here for a while, then go to Tusculum.

P.S. When he was passing Dolabella's house, he mounted and
paraded the whole of his armed guard to right and left, a thing he did
nowhere else. I had this from Nicias.          (*Ad Att.*, XIII, 52)

*To Manius Curius, at Patras*                    *Rome, January,* 44 B.C.
No, I certainly no longer urge or even ask you to return home. On
the contrary, I long to fly away myself and get to some place

> Far from the madding crowd's ignoble strife.

You can't imagine how disgracefully I feel I am behaving in being
party to what is going on. You do seem to have foreseen much earlier
what was impending, at the time when you got away from Rome. It
may be painful to hear of these things, but hearing is more tolerable
than seeing. At least you weren't on the Field of Mars when this
happened. The proceedings for the election of quaestors were begun
at 8.0 a.m. The official chair of Quintus Maximus, whom the Caesarians
declared to be consul, had been set in place, but was removed again on
the announcement that he was dead. Then Caesar, though he had

performed the ceremonies proper to introduce a quaestorial election, proceeded to treat the meeting as if it were for a consular election, and at one o'clock announced the election of a consul to serve until January 1, which was next morning. So I can inform you that in Caninius' consulship no one had lunch.[1] Still, nothing untoward occurred while he was consul: such was his vigilance that throughout his consulship he did not sleep a wink!

Yes, you may laugh, but you aren't here. If you were, you could not help weeping. What if I told you everything? There are countless similar instances. I could not endure it if I had not sought shelter in the haven of philosophy and got my dear Atticus as companion in my studies. You say you belong to him by right of legal ownership and contract, but to me by right of usufruct; well, I'm quite content with that, since what a man uses and enjoys can most truly be called his. But more of this another time.

Acilius, who has been sent to Greece with the troops, is under a very great obligation to me, since I have twice successfully defended him in a trial in which his citizenship was at stake, and being not ungrateful by nature he shows a strong regard for me. I have written him a very full letter about you and sent it by the same post as this. Please let me know how he has taken it and what he has promised to do for you.                                    (*Ad Fam.*, VII, 30)

---

1. Lunch would be over by 1 p.m. and his consulship at midnight. Caesar was degrading the consular office by giving it to a friend for less than a day, as a reward for services rendered.

# 44 to 43 B.C.

*In 46 and 45 Caesar had been carrying out a great programme of reform, including the improvement of social services, the planting of colonies, the admission to the Senate of freedman's sons and even of provincial notables, and the correction of the calendar, which necessitated the insertion of 67 extra days between November and December, 46. But he was ruling as Dictator, and the chief offices of State were held by his nominees.*

*Cicero had at first been hopeful that Caesar would eventually restore free institutions, and said as much in a speech he delivered, his first for six years, in 46. But it gradually became clear that he had no such intentions. There is no evidence that he encouraged people to believe him a god, but his toleration, even of what happened in the procession, was sure to shock men like Cicero. Hitherto he had shown admiration for Caesar's moderation, though little appreciation of his genius as an administrator. He now became more bitter. Nevertheless he was not one of those who were approached early in 44 by Brutus and Cassius.*

*The events that followed are well-known from Shakespeare's* Julius Caesar, *based on Plutarch's account. Two tribunes, Flavius and Marullus, removed a diadem which had been placed on Caesar's statue, and on January 26 arrested the ringleaders of a crowd which hailed him as king. Caesar deprecated the title, but attacked the two champions of republicanism, who were deposed by an obsequious Senate. Three weeks later, probably by collusion and in order to allay suspicion, Antony at the Feast of the Lupercalia offered him a kingly diadem, which he ostentatiously refused. He was due to leave shortly to campaign against Parthia, and an old prophecy was now unearthed which was interpreted to mean that*

*only under a king would the Romans conquer the Parthians. The psycho-
logical moment for the republican conspirators had come.*

*On the Ides of March, despite threatening omens, Caesar took his
seat in the Senate House. Trebonius drew Antony aside, the conspirators
closed in with their daggers, and he fell riddled with wounds at the foot
of Pompey's statue.*

*After the murder the tyrannicides ran out brandishing their weapons
and shouting Cicero's name. Later they withdrew to the top of the Capitol.
We do not know whether Cicero was in the Senate House that day, but
he visited them in the evening. Next day Dolabella became Antony's
colleague as consul; and on the day after, the Feast of the Liberalia, when
the Senate met again, Cicero supported an amnesty and apparently did
not oppose the ratification of Caesar's acts, which was part of what
purported to be a general settlement.*

*Antony now established his ascendancy. He read Caesar's will, with its
popular legacies, to the crowd, and burnt his body on a pyre in the Forum,
himself pronouncing a moving funeral oration (Shakespeare's 'Friends,
Romans, Countrymen . . .' speech).*

*To Brutus and Cassius, on the Capitol,          Rome, March 17, 44 B.C.
from Decimus Brutus.*[1]

Our situation is as follows. Hirtius was at my house yesterday
evening; he made it clear to me what Antony's intentions were—evil
and treacherous in the extreme; he had said that he could not let me
have my province, and that he did not think any of us could safely
remain in the Capital in view of the unrest among the troops and the
masses. I am sure you will realise that both these contentions are false
and that the truth is to be found in what Hirtius made clear, namely
that Antony is afraid that, if our position received even moderate
support, there would be no part left for them to play on the political
stage.

In this awkward situation I decided to request a nominal mission
abroad for myself and our colleagues, by way of finding a decent excuse
for leaving Rome. Hirtius promised to obtain this, but I am confident
that he will; there is so much arrogance and hostility towards us in

1. Decimus Brutus (called 'Decius' by Shakespeare) was Governor-designate
of the Po Valley (Hither Gaul). He was not with the other conspirators on the
Capitol, but had returned to his own house.

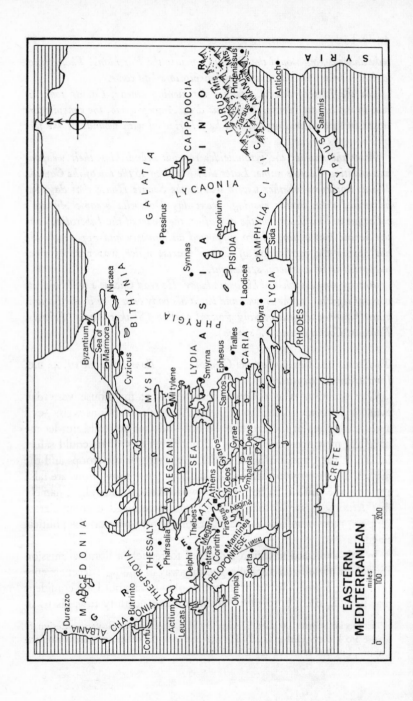

EASTERN
MEDITERRANEAN

miles
0    100    200

SYRIA

Antioch

Salamis
CYPRUS

TAURUS Mts
? Pindenissus
Tarsus
AMANUS Mts
Mt.
CILICIA
PAMPHYLIA
Sida

CAPPADOCIA

LYCAONIA
Iconium
Pessinus
PISIDIA
Laodicea
LYCIA
Cibyra

GALATIA

Synnas
MINO
A
S
I
A

PHRYGIA
RHODES

BITHYNIA
Nicaea
Sea of
Marmora
Byzantium
Cyzicus
MYSIA
Mitylene
LYDIA
Smyrna
Samos
Ephesus
Tralles
CARIA
Gyaros
Gyrae
Delos
Lombarda
Ceos
Athens
ATT
Megara
Piraeus
Aegina
Mantinea
PELOPONNESE
Olympia
Sparta

CRETE

AEGEAN
SEA

THESSALY
Pharsalia
Delphi
Thebes
Patras
Corinth

MACEDONIA
EPIRUS
CHA
Butrinto
ONIA
THESPROTIA
Actium
Leucas
Corfu
ALBANIA
Durazzo
G
R
E

the air. And even if they grant our request, I think that before long we shall find ourselves declared public enemies or outlaws.

You want to know what I advise? We must yield to fate; I think we must clear out of Italy and emigrate to Rhodes or somewhere. If things get better, we can return to Rome; if no worse, we can live in exile; if worse, we can have recourse to extreme measures.

Here perhaps one of you will ask, why wait for the last stage rather than make an effort of some sort now? The answer is that we have no rallying-points except Sextus Pompey[1] and Caecilius Bassus,[2] who will gain in strength, I expect, when the news about Caesar arrives. It will be time enough to join them when we have found out how strong they are.

On behalf of yourself and Cassius I will give any undertaking you wish: Hirtius insists that I do so. I must ask you to answer this letter as soon as possible, since I have no doubt he will let me know about my request by ten o'clock; please say where we can meet, that is to say, where you would like me to come.

P.S. Since my last conversation with Hirtius I have decided to ask for us to be allowed a State-provided bodyguard while we are at Rome. I don't expect they will agree; we should be putting them so very much in the wrong. But I thought I ought to make any request I considered fair. *(Ad Fam.,* XI, I)[3]

*To Atticus, at Rome    c/o Gaius Matius, near Rome, April 7, 44 B.C.*
I am stopping with the man we talked of yesterday. Quite desperate, his tone was: 'no chance of a solution. If Caesar with all his genius could find no way out, who will now?' In fact he says that all is lost. It may well be so but he seems so pleased about it, and is positive that within three weeks there will be a rising in Gaul. He says he hasn't discussed the situation since the Ides of March with anyone but Lepidus. His conclusion is that a crisis like this can't just pass off. How much wiser Oppius is! He regrets Caesar's death quite as much, but says nothing that could offend any loyalist. But enough of this.

1. Younger son of Pompey the Great. He was still at large in Spain with some troops.
2. Leader of a revolt against the Caesarians in Syria, which succeeded with help from Parthia.
3. From a copy presumably sent to Cicero 'for information' by the conspirators.

Please, if there is any news (and I expect plenty), don't be slack about writing; for instance, whether we can rely on Sextus Pompey, and particularly about Marcus Brutus, of whom my host alleges that Caesar used to say: 'It makes all the difference what that man wants; but whatever he wants, he wants it passionately'; and that he had noticed this when Brutus pleaded for Deiotarus at Nicaea, how intensely and unrestrainedly he spoke.

And by the way (since I like to put down anything that comes into my head), Matius says that when not long ago I called on Caesar at Sestius' request and was sitting outside waiting to be called in, Caesar remarked: 'How can I doubt that I am most unpopular, seeing that Marcus Cicero has to sit out there and cannot have access to me whenever he wants? And yet there is no one so good natured as he is. Still, I have little doubt that he hates me like poison.' He has told me a lot else besides.

But to the point again. Any news, great or small, let me have it. And I on my side will let nothing escape me.     (*Ad Att.*, XIV, 1)

*To Atticus, at Rome          Lanuvium, near Velletri, April* 10, 44 B.C.

What news should I hear at Lanuvium? But at Rome I suspect you hear something fresh every day. Things are coming to a head; for if Matius talks like that, what must the other Caesarians be saying? What worries me is that, contrary to all precedent elsewhere, the recovery of freedom has not meant the revival of the constitution. It is terrifying to hear what people are saying and threatening. I'm also afraid there may be a rising in Gaul, and that Sextus Pompey himself may jump the wrong way.

But come one, come all, the Ides of March console me. What our heroes could do, of themselves, they accomplished most gloriously and magnificently. The sequel requires funds and forces, and we have neither.

That's all I have to tell you. If you hear any news (and I expect some daily) let me have it straight away; and if no news, still don't let us break our custom of regularly exchanging notes. I will see I don't.

(*Ad Att.*, XIV, 4)

*To Atticus, at Rome          Pozzuoli, near Naples, April* 18, 44 B.C.

I learnt a lot about the state of affairs from your letters, a whole string of which were handed me together by Vestorius' freedman.

I'll answer your questions briefly. I am delighted with the property Cluvius has left me. Why did I have in the architect Chrysippus? Because two of my cottages have collapsed and the rest have got cracks, so that not only have the tenants moved out, but even the mice. Others would call this a disaster; to me it's not even a nuisance. O Socrates and all the tribe of Socrates, how shall I ever thank you enough? God, how little I bother about such things! However, building has begun on the advice and prompting of Vestorius, designed to turn my loss into gain.

There's a big crowd here, and I understand it will be bigger. It includes two so-called consuls-designate.[1] Good Lord! The tyrant dead, the tyranny lives on! We are celebrating the death of a man whose acts we are defending. So Marcus Curtius is arraigning us so sternly that we are ashamed to be alive, and no wonder. For to die would have been a thousand times better than to live through all this, which looks like becoming chronic.

Balbus is here too, and often with me. He had a letter from Vetus, dated December 31, to say that when he was besieging Caecilius and was on the point of catching him, Pacorus the Parthian had turned up with a very large force; so Caecilius was snatched from him, and he suffered considerable casualties. He puts the blame on Volcacius. So war seems to be blowing up in that quarter. But let's leave that to Dolabella and Nicias.

Balbus had better news of Gaul, a letter dated three weeks back saying that the Germans and those peoples, on hearing about Caesar, sent delegates to Aurelius, who had been put in charge by Hirtius, to say that they would carry out his orders. You see? Peace reigns every-were, and Matius was wrong.                (*Ad Att.*, xiv, 9)

*To Atticus, at Rome*          *Cuma, near Naples, April* 19, 44 B.C.
Has it come to this? Is this all our hero Brutus has achieved, that he should have to stay at Lanuvium, and that Trebonius should slink off to his province by a roundabout route? And that all the acts, memoranda, speeches, promises and thoughts of Caesar should have more validity now than if he were himself still living? Do you remember how on that very first day on the Capitol I lifted up my voice in favour of the praetors calling a meeting of the Senate on the Capitol?

1. Hirtius and Pansa, selected by Caesar for 43 B.C.

F

Good heavens, what things could then have been accomplished, when all good and even fairly good patriots were rejoicing, and the gangsters were broken! You blame what we did on the Liberalia.[1] But what could have been done then? We were already finished long before. Do you remember how you shouted that our cause was lost if Caesar's funeral took place? Yet he was cremated in the Forum itself, and a moving funeral oration was delivered in his praise,[2] and slaves and beggars were despatched with firebrands to attack our houses.[3] And the next thing is, they have the face to say: 'Do you dare oppose the will of Caesar?' This and suchlike things are more than I can bear. So my thoughts are turning to 'from land to land', but your Greek land is too exposed to the blast. . . .                  (*Ad Att.*, xiv, 10, 1)

*By April there had returned to Italy Octavius, Caesar's eighteen-year-old great-nephew, the future Augustus. His posthumous adoption by Caesar had not yet been ratified, but he had no intention of abandoning his position. Some Caesarians rallied to him, but when Antony scouted his claims, he decided to use Cicero and the Republicans as his ladder. Cicero meanwhile had avoided any open breach with the Caesarians, even with Antony.*

*To Atticus, at Rome*        Pozzuoli, near Naples, April 22, 44 b.c.
    O my dear Atticus, I am much afraid that the Ides of March may have given us nothing but the rejoicing and the satisfaction of our hatred and indignation. What news I get from Rome! And what things I see here!

Fair was the deed, but only half complete.

You know how devoted I am to the Sicilians, and how proud I am to have been chosen their patron. Caesar gave them many privileges, and I had no objection, except that to grant them the rights of Latins

1. The second day after the Ides of March, when the Senate met and decreed that Caesar's acts be confirmed, his will read, and his funeral held in public. Cicero himself spoke then in favour of an amnesty, hence his apologetic tone here.

2. By Mark Antony. Cf. Shakespeare, *J.C.* iii, ii, 78 ff: 'Friends, Romans, countrymen . . .'.

3. Ib. 260 ff. and iii.

was altogether too much. However . . . Now, lo and behold, Mark
Antony, in return for a huge bribe, has promulgated a decree alleged
to have been carried in the Assembly by the Dictator, making the
Sicilians Roman Citizens; of which in Caesar's lifetime there had been
no word. . . .

With me here, and treating me with great deference and great
friendliness, is Octavius. His companions are greeting him as 'Caesar',
but Philippus[1] does not, so neither do I, and I maintain that no loyal
citizen can. There are so many around him who are breathing slaughter
against our friends; they say the situation is intolerable. What do you
think will happen when the boy arrives at Rome, where our liberators
cannot live in safety? Glorious these will always be, indeed even happy
in the consciousness of what they have done. But unless I am mistaken, our side will go under. And so I am eager to get away anywhere 'far from the madding crowd'. I am not at all pleased even with
these consuls-elect,[2] who have actually made me coach them in
oratory, so that I have no peace even at the seaside. But that is my
fault for being too bad at refusing. There was a time when I more or
less had to do such jobs, but now, however things turn out, it is no
longer so.

What ages it is since I had anything to tell you. But I am writing
not so much to please you with *my* letter as to elicit one from you.
Tell me any news there is about the others, and every scrap about
Brutus. I am writing this on April 22 while dining with Vestorius, a
man with much experience of bookkeeping but no notion of
philosophy.                                    (*Ad Att.*, XIV, 12)

*To Atticus, at Rome*          *Pozzuoli, near Naples, April 26,* 44 B.C.
. . . Mark Antony has written to me about the recall of Sextus
Clodius. You will see from the copy I enclose how complimentary to
myself its terms are, but you will also easily perceive how unprincipled,
disgraceful and mischievous the proposal is. No wonder that at times
one almost wishes Caesar were still here. Things he would never have
done or allowed are now proposed on the strength of memoranda
fraudulently produced as his.

However, I have made no difficulty at all about it to Antony. For

1. Octavius' step-father.
2. Hirtius and Pansa.

having once got it into his head that he could do what he liked, he would have done it all the same even if I had objected. So I enclose a copy of my reply as well. (*Ad Att.*, XIV, 13, 6)

*To Cicero, at Pozzuoli, from Mark Antony,* ?*Rome, April* 24, 44 B.C. *Consul*

I was prevented by pressure of work and by your sudden departure from mentioning to you personally a request which I am afraid may carry less weight with you in my absence. But if your kindness confirms the opinion I have always had of you, I shall be very glad.

Some time ago I petitioned Caesar to recall Sextus Clodius[1] from exile, and he consented. My intention even at the time was only to avail myself of this favour if you did not object. So I am all the more anxious now to be allowed to do so with your kind permission. If, however, you show yourself unmoved by his wretched and forlorn plight, I shall not dispute the matter with you, although I think my duty is to carry out any memorandum of Caesar's.

But really, if you want to show a generous, wise and friendly attitude towards me, you will of course be indulgent; and you will also wish young Publius Clodius, a boy of the highest promise, to take note that you did not persecute his father's friends when you had the chance. Do please, I beg you, let it be seen that your feud with his father arose from political motives, and don't show contempt for his family. For there is more honour and less reluctance in giving up quarrels arising from political causes than those arising from personal injury. So let me have a chance to inculcate this lesson and impress upon the boy's receptive mind that quarrels should not be handed down from one generation to another.

I am well aware, my dear Cicero, that your fortunes are now beyond the reach of danger, but yet I think you would prefer your old age to be full of peace and honour rather than anxiety. And finally, I think I have a right to ask this favour of you, since I have done everything I could in your interest. If I do not obtain it, I shall not take it upon myself to recall Clodius, so that you may be aware of my respect for your authority and may therefore be the more ready to relent.

(Enclosure: *Ad Att.*, XIV, 13A)

---

1. A hanger-on of the Clodius who got Cicero banished in 58 B.C.

*To Atticus, at Rome*                    *Pozzuoli, near Naples, May* 2, 44 B.C.

I'm sending this off on May 2, just as I'm going aboard a pinnace at Cluvius' gardens, after handing over the house on the Lucrine Lake to your wife, including the foremen and staff. For my part, I'm threatening to descend today on Paetus' stock-fish *au gratin*. In a few days' time I shall go to my place at Pompeii, and then sail back to my domains at Pozzuoli and Cuma. How very attractive these places are in every respect save for the crowds of visitors, which almost compel one to avoid them.

But to come to the point, what a doughty deed of our Dolabella's.[1] What an eye-opener it will be! I keep on praising and encouraging him. I fully agree with all you have said in your letters about him and about his action. It seems to me our Brutus could now safely walk through the Forum even with a golden crown on his head; for who would dare to touch him with the cross or the precipice before their eyes, especially when the lower orders have given such applause and approval to the deed.

Now, my dear Atticus, do help me out. I am anxious, as soon as I have done all that Brutus requires of me, to run over to Greece. It is very important for Marcus, or rather myself, and indeed for both of us, that I should look in on him at his studies. For do you think the letter you sent me from his tutor Leonides contains much cause for satisfaction? I shall never be satisfied with any report on him which qualifies praise with 'if he keeps it up'. That suggests anxiety, not confidence. Again, I instructed another of his teachers, Herodes, to write me detailed reports, but so far he has not sent a word. I'm afraid he may have had nothing to tell me which he thought I should be glad to hear.

Many thanks for writing to Xeno. My duty and my reputation alike require that Marcus should not be short of anything. . . .

(*Ad Att.*, XIV, 16)

*To Atticus, at Rome*                       *Astura, near Anzio, May* 19, 44 B.C.

I must say, this is a pretty place; sequestered, at any rate, and free from people hanging over you, if you want to write. Yet somehow or other 'there's no place like home'. So I'm continually drawn to

---

1. He had demolished a memorial erected in Caesar's honour in the Forum by some of his supporters and had the ringleaders crucified or thrown off the Tarpeian Rock.

Tusculum. And after all, one will probably soon get tired of the picturesqueness of this bit of coast. Besides, I'm afraid of rain myself, unless my weather-signs deceive me: the frogs are holding forth.

Please let me know where and when I can see Brutus.

*(Ad Att.*, XV, 16A)

*To Cicero, from Trebonius*          *Athens, May* 25, 44 B.C.

I trust you are well. I arrived at Athens on May 22 and there, as I had very much hoped, I saw your son, and found him absorbed in the most improving studies and very well spoken of for steadiness. I need not tell you how much pleasure that gave me, since you are well aware how much you mean to me and how sincere friendship of a long standing makes me rejoice in the least bit of happiness you have, let alone in so great a blessing as this. Don't think, my dear Cicero, that I'm only telling you this to cheer you up: nothing could be more popular with all those who are in residence at Athens or more devoted to the pursuits that you love most (which means, the best) than your young man—or may I call him *ours*, since your interests and mine are inseparable? So I am delighted to congratulate you, as I can with all sincerity, and myself no less, because he whom we would be bound to love whatever his character proves to possess a character we can love spontaneously.

In the course of conversation he remarked that he would like to visit Asia Minor, whereupon I not only invited him but pressed him to do so, above all during my governorship. You must not doubt that I will look after him with the same loving care as you would as his father. I shall also make sure that his philosophy tutor, Cratippus, accompanies him, in case you should think he was going to take a holiday in Asia Minor from the studies you are so keen that he should pursue. For though I can see he is fully prepared and has already got into his stride, I shall not omit to spur him on to making progress day by day in his learning and his exercises. . . .

You will, I am sure, fulfil your promise and get me into one of your dialogues as soon as possible. If you write anything about Caesar's death, I am sure you will not fail to emphasise my share both in the deed[1] and in your affection.

1. All he had done was to detain Antony in conversation while the others stabbed Caesar.

I am relying on you to look after my mother and family.

*(Ad Fam.,* XII, 16, 1–2; 4)

*To Mark Antony, Consul*                    *Lanuvium, near Velletri,*
*from Brutus and Cassius, Praetors*              *end of May,* 44 B.C.

We should not have written you this letter if we were not convinced of your good faith and good will towards us; and this being your attitude, we are sure you will take it in good part.

We have been informed that a large crowd of ex-servicemen has already collected at Rome, and that it will be greatly increased by June 1.[1] It would be unworthy of us to entertain any doubts or fears with regard to you. But since we have put ourselves in your hands and in deference to your advice have dismissed our supporters from the provincial towns, not only by our edict but by personal letters, we surely deserve to share your counsels, especially in a matter that affects ourselves. Accordingly we beg you to inform us of your intentions towards us. Do you think we shall be safe amid such a crowd of ex-servicemen, who are even thinking, we hear, of re-erecting the memorial to Caesar demolished by Dolabella, an action which we believe no one could desire or countenance who had the interests of our safety and reputation at heart.

Events have proved that from the first we had an eye only to peace, and sought nothing save freedom for all. No one can cheat us save you, and to do so would clearly be foreign to your high principles and integrity; no one else has the means of deceiving us, for it is you, and you alone, that we have trusted and shall continue to trust.

Our friends are extremely alarmed about us. They are convinced by experience of your own good faith, but they cannot help reflecting that a crowd of ex-servicemen can more easily be driven by others in any direction they like than held in check by you. We ask you for a detailed explanation, since the suggestion is quite frivolous and worthless that a summons has been issued to ex-servicemen because you were intending to bring up a proposal affecting their interests some time in June. Who do you think is likely to obstruct you, since it is definite that our attitude will be passive? No one has a right to

1. Antony had been busy for a month collecting them from all over Italy against the meeting of the Senate on June 1.

accuse us of undue love of life, seeing that nothing could happen to us without universal ruin and chaos ensuing.        (*Ad Fam.*, XI, 2)[1]

*To Atticus, at Rome*                    *Tusculum, near Rome, June* 2, 44 B.C.

On the evening of June 2 I got a letter from Balbus saying that there would be a meeting of the Senate on the 5th to appoint Brutus to Asia Minor and Cassius to Sicily as commissioners for buying corn and despatching it to Rome. What a humiliation! Fancy being given any post by the Caesarians, let alone one that a subordinate minister could fill! Still, perhaps it's better than sitting by the Eurotas. But fate must have its way. Balbus says also that a decree will be passed at the same time nominating them and the other ex-praetors as governors of provinces next year. At least a province is better than that Persian Pavilion (don't mistake me: the Spartan features I mention are no further away than Lanuvium[2]). How can I joke about such serious things? Well, what else can I do? I'm tired of lamenting. . . .        (*Ad Att.*, XV, 9, 1)

*To Atticus, at Rome*                                      *Anzio, June* 8, 44 B.C.

I got to Anzio on the 8th. Brutus was delighted to see me. Then in front of Servilia, Tertia and Portia[3] and many others he asked me my opinion. Favonius was among them. I had thought over on the way what I should say, and advised him to accept the post in Asia Minor: there was nothing left for us to do but make sure of his safety; while he was safe there was hope for the Republic.

I was in the middle of my argument when in came Cassius. I went over the ground again. Whereupon his eyes flashed and as though breathing fire and slaughter he declared he would not go to Sicily: was he to accept an insult as a favour? 'Then what are you going to do?' I asked. He said he would go to Greece. 'What about you, Brutus?' I said. 'To Rome, if you advise it.' 'Certainly not: you'll not be safe.' 'Well, if I could be safe, would you approve?' 'In so far as I don't think you ought to take a province either now or after your praetorship. But I can't advise you to trust yourself in Rome.' I added the reasons, which will of course occur to you, why he would not be safe there.

1. Presumably a copy sent to Cicero 'for information' by Brutus and Cassius.

2. Brutus' grounds at Lanuvium were laid out as a mock-Sparta, complete with River Eurotas and Persian Pavilion. Cf. Hadrian's Villa near Tivoli.

3. Brutus' mother, half-sister and wife respectively.

Then they bewailed for a long time, especially Cassius, the chances they had let slip, and severely criticised Decimus Brutus. I said we ought not to rake up the past, but I could not help agreeing. When I had begun to say what ought to have been done—nothing new, but what everyone says daily—and while refraining from making my old point that someone besides Caesar ought to have been touched,[1] declared that the Senate should have been summoned, the popular enthusiasm still further fanned and the whole government taken over by the tyrannicides, your friend Servilia exclaimed, 'Well, I never heard anyone . . .' but I would not let her finish.

My impression was, however, that Cassius will go (Servilia promised she would see that the commissionership for corn was omitted from the bill), and our friend Brutus soon dropped his silly talk about wanting to go to Rome. He has made up his mind accordingly to let the festival be given in his name without his being present.[2] But it looks as if he wants to sail for Asia Minor from Anzio.

To sum up, I got no satisfaction from my journey except a good conscience. I could not allow Brutus to leave Italy without my having an interview with him; but apart from the discharging of this debt to duty and affection, I could not help asking myself

Prophet, what profit hath thy journey now?

The fact is, the ship I found was breaking up, or rather already broken in pieces. No plan, no principle, no system. So although I had no doubts even before, I am all the more determined to fly away from here, and that as soon as possible

Far from the madding crowd's ignoble strife.

And by the way, listen to this: Dolabella chose me on the 5th as one of his deputies. I got the news yesterday evening. Even you did not like the idea of a pilgrimage to fulfil a vow; and indeed it was absurd for me to be fulfilling a vow made for the preservation of the constitution when the constitution has been overthrown.[3] Besides, I

1. i.e. Antony.
2. Brutus wanted to go to Rome partly because, as Praetor of the City, it was his privilege to preside over the Festival of Apollo in July, an opportunity for gauging, if not winning, popularity.
3. Cicero had been looking for an excuse to go abroad.

believe such sinecure missions have a time limit set by one of Caesar's laws, and cannot easily be extended. What I want is a mission that will let me come and go as I please, and that I have now obtained. And it will be very nice to have this privilege for five years. However, why think of five years hence? I fancy things are coming to a head. But *absit omen.*                                                                (*Ad Att.*, XV, 11)

*To Atticus, at Rome*                                        *Anzio, June* 11, 44 B.C.

Post from young Marcus at last, and what do you think? A letter written in brocaded phrases, which in itself indicates some progress. And besides, his reports from the others are splendid. Leonides, it is true, still says 'so far'; but Herodes' is 'excellent' without qualification. Ah well! This is a matter on which I'm even glad to have dust thrown in my eyes, and content to be credulous.

Please let me know if you hear anything from Statius that concerns me.                                                                     (*Ad Att.*, XV, 16)

*To Atticus, at Rome*                                  *Astura, near Anzio, June* 13, 44 B.C.

... I hate the Queen;[1] and the man who vouches for her promises, Ammonius, knows I have good reason to do so; not but what the gifts she promised were of a literary nature and not beneath my dignity—the sort I should not have minded proclaiming in public. Her man Sara too, besides being a rogue, I have found impertinent towards myself. Once, and once only, have I seen him in my house; and then, when I asked him politely what he wanted, he said he was looking for Atticus! The Queen's insolence, too, when she was living in Caesar's house in the gardens beyond the Tiber, I cannot recall without indignation. So no dealings with that lot. They seem to think I have not only no spirit, but no feelings at all.

My departure from Italy is held up by the way Eros manages my affairs; for whereas according to the audit he made on April 5 I ought to have plenty in hand, I am being obliged to borrow; and as for the receipts from those rents, I thought I had ear-marked them for that shrine. But I've handed over the matter to Tiro, and sent him to Rome for that purpose; I didn't want to burden you with it when you are already overburdened.

1. Cleopatra. She had stayed at Rome under Caesar's protection since the summer of 46, and had fled soon after his assassination. Cicero can now speak his mind about her. We do not know for what favour she was angling.

The reticence of dear Marcus about his wants makes me all the more worried about them. He never said a word about them to me, the first person he should have approached; but he wrote to Tiro that since April 1, the end of his financial year, he had received no allowance. Now I know that, being you, you have always agreed with the view that my position demanded that he should be treated by me not merely liberally, but handsomely and lavishly. So please arrange (I should not trouble you if I could do it through anyone else) for him to have a bill of exchange at Athens for his whole year's allowance. Eros will of course reimburse you. I have sent Tiro to see about it.

Please go into this and let me know any views you have on the subject.                                             (*Add Att.*, XV, 15, 2–4)

*To Trebatius,*[1] *at Rome*            *Tusculum, near Rome, ? June,* 44 B.C.
You made fun of me yesterday over the wine for saying that it was a disputed point whether an heir could lawfully prosecute for an embezzlement committed before he succeeded to the inheritance. So although I got home late and mellow, I marked the section dealing with this dispute and now enclose a copy of it, to show you that the view you said no one had taken was held by Sextus Aelius, Manius Manilius and Marcus Brutus. All the same I concur myself with Scaevola and Trebatius.                              (*Ad Fam.*, VII, 22)

*To Atticus, at Rome*            *Pozzuoli, near Naples, July* 9, 44 B.C.
Brutus is waiting for a letter from you. I told him what happened during Accius' *Tereus*, but he knew already. (He thought it was the *Brutus*).[2] On the other hand there was some breath of rumour that the opening of the Greek performances had been badly attended, which didn't surprise me at all. You know what I think of Greek shows.

Now for the most important thing of all. My nephew Quintus has been with me for several days, and would have stayed even longer if I had wanted it. But throughout his visit you wouldn't believe how delighted I was with him in every way and especially where he used

1. The prominent lawyer (see pp. 64 and 65). He was later a friend of Horace.
2. At the festival given in Brutus' name there had been some popular demonstration during this play. Brutus was anxious to hear from Atticus how his festival was going down.

to disappoint me.[1] He was so completely changed, partly by some writings I was engaged on, partly by my constantly talking to him and lecturing him, that in future his political attitude will be such as we wish. After he had not only promised me this but also convinced me of his sincerity, he pressed me earnestly at great length to guarantee to you that he would live up to your expectations and mine, saying that he was not asking that you should trust him immediately, but that you should take him to your heart only when you had seen for yourself. If he had not convinced me, and if I had not decided that what I am telling you would last, I would not have done what I am going to tell you. I took the young man with me to Brutus. He was so much in agreement with what I have been saying to you that he believed it independently and would have no guarantee from me. After praising Quintus and mentioning you in very friendly terms, he sent him off with a kiss and an embrace. So although I have more reason to congratulate you than ask you a favour, still I will ask you to make up your mind that Quintus has put behind him any irregularities due to the unsteadiness of youth that used to appear in his conduct, and to believe me when I say that your influence will contribute much, everything in fact, towards confirming him in his good resolutions.

I gave Brutus frequent hints about our sailing together, but he does not seem to jump at the idea as I thought he would. I thought him rather *distrait*, and by Jove he was, especially about the Festival. And when I got home Gnaeus Lucceius, who is on intimate terms with him, said that he was hesitating a good deal, not because he was backing out, but in the hope that something would turn up. So I am wondering whether to make for Venosa and there await news about those legions.[2] If, as some think, they will not be there, I shall go to Otranto; but if both that and Brindisi are unsafe, I shall come back here. You think I'm not serious? I swear you're the only person who keeps me here. . . .

As to my letters, there is no collection in existence, but Tiro has about seventy, and some can be recovered from you. I ought to look

---

1. Probably he had been too close to Antony, as he had been before to Caesar. In the previous year he had behaved very badly, traducing his uncle, running into debt, pretending to quarrel with his mother and later refusing to accept a step-mother.

2. Coming from Macedonia to reinforce Antony.

over these and correct them; they shall not be published until I have
done so.[1]                                     (*Ad Att.*, XVI, 5, 1–3, 5)

*To Atticus, at Rome*           *Pompeii, near Naples, July* 17, 44 B.C.
At long last I'm answering the letter you sent me after meeting
Antony's brother Lucius at Tivoli. It was sensible of you, it certainly
was, to give in and even to volunteer your thanks. For as you say,
we shall part company with the constitution sooner than with our
property.[2]
You increase my keenness to write by saying you enjoy my work
*On Old Age* more and more every day. You say you expect Eros not
to come back to you empty-handed, and I am glad you will not be
disappointed; but it is the same essay I am sending you in a revised
form, in fact the original itself with many interlinear additions and
corrections. Get a fair copy made on large paper and read it out
privately to your guests, but, please, for my sake, do it when they are
in a good temper and have dined well, otherwise they may vent on me
their dissatisfaction with you. . . .                   (*Ad Att.*, XVI, 3, 1)

*To Atticus, at Rome*        *Vibo Valentia, Toe of Italy, July* 25, 44 B.C.
Up to now, having got as far as Sicca's house at Vibo, I've been
travelling with more comfort than energy. Mostly rowing, no nor'-
nor'-easters. That has been lucky, as we have had two bays to cross,
those of Paestum and Vibo. We crossed both with the wind behind.
So I got to Sicca's place on the eighth day after leaving Pompeii. I
stopped one day on the way at Elea, where I put up very comfortably
at Talna's, and could not have had a warmer welcome, especially as he
was away himself. So I reached Sicca's on the 24th, and here I feel so
much at home that I'm staying on a day extra.
When I get to Reggio I think I shall have to consider, since I am
'bound far across the seas', whether to take a cargo-boat to Patras or
go by packet-boat to the Leucopetra near Taranto and cross from

1. It need not be assumed from this that Cicero ever did correct them, or that
he intended all the letters to be published rather than a selection of the more
polished; certainly not that he wrote them for publication.
2. Atticus had not opposed Lucius Antony's project of confiscating lands at
Tivoli for redistribution, but had concentrated on persuading him to exempt
Cicero's estate there.

there to Corfu; and if I decide on a merchant-ship, whether to go
directly from the Straits or pick one up at Syracuse. I'll write and tell
you about this from Reggio.

Upon my word, Atticus, I often ask myself

What profit hath thy journey now?

Why am I not with you? Why have I deprived my eyes of the jewels
of Italy, my houses? It's more than enough objection that I am not
with you. But what am I running away from? Danger? At the moment
at least there's none, unless I'm mistaken. The danger will be at the
time when you want me to return, saying that people are full of praise
for my leaving, provided only that I return before January 1,[1] which
I shall certainly endeavour to do. I'd rather be in trepidation at home
than in no trepidation at your Athens. But keep your eye on the way
things are going and either write, or better still, bring the news
yourself. . . .

Now I have a piece of carelessness to confess. My book *On Glory*
that I sent you had the same exordium as the Third Book of my
*Academica*. The explanation is this: I keep a volume of exordia, and
my practice is to select one for any work I have taken in hand. So
being at Tusculum at the time and not remembering that I had used
up that one, I put it into the book I sent you. I only discovered my
mistake while re-reading the *Academica* on the boat. So I dashed off
a new exordium at once and have sent it to you. You can detach the
other and stick this on instead.

Please give my love to Pilia and Attica, both great favourites
of mine.                                    (*Ad Att.*, XVI, 6, 1–2; 4)

*To Mark Antony, Consul,*                    *Naples, August* 4, 44 B.C.
*from Brutus and Cassius*
Sir,

We have received your letter, which was of a piece with your
manifesto, arrogant, threatening, and by no means such as should
have been sent to us by you. We have done you no injury, Antony,
to provoke this, and we did not believe that you would be surprised if
praetors or men of our standing requested something from a consul

1. When Hirtius and Pansa would succeed Antony and Dolabella as consuls.

in a manifesto. But if you are indignant that we ventured to do so, you will permit us to regret that you personally would not concede even so small a privilege to a Brutus or a Cassius. We do not question your protestation that it was in all good faith that you denied ever complaining of our raising troops, requisitioning money, tampering with legions and despatching emissaries overseas, but neither do we acknowledge the truth of any of these allegations; and we are surprised that, if you passed this over in silence, a fit of anger should have betrayed you into reproaching us with the death of Caesar.

Reflect, please, whether this is a tolerable situation, that praetors should not be allowed, for the sake of harmony and liberty, to waive one of their rights[1] by edict without threat of arms from a consul. Your reliance on this has no terrors for us; for it is not right or proper that our spirit should be cowed by any danger, nor that Antony should claim authority over those to whose efforts he owes his own liberty.

If we had other motives for stirring up civil war, your letter would have no effect on us; for free men are not impressed by a blusterer. But you know full well that we cannot be driven in any direction, and perhaps your threatening attitude is designed to make our considered policy look like fear.

It remains our desire that you should be prominent and respected in a free State; we challenge you to no feuds, while still valuing our liberty more than your friendship. Think over again and again what you are undertaking and what you can carry off, and fix your mind not on how long Caesar lived, but on how long he did not reign. God grant that your deliberations prove conducive to the safety of the Republic and of yourself; failing that, we pray that they may be as little injurious to yourself as is compatible the Republic's welfare and honour.                                              (*Ad Fam.*, XI, 3)[2]

*To Atticus, at Rome*               *At sea, off Pompeii, August 19, 44 B.C.*
After I had started on August 6 from Leucopetra (I was crossing from there) and gone about forty miles, a strong south wind arose and blew me back there again. While I was waiting for a favourable wind

1. The right to be in Rome. Brutus and Cassius had announced, to avoid causing dissension, that they would go straight to their provinces.
2. Copy presumably sent to Cicero 'for information' by Brutus and Cassius.

(our friend Valerius has a house there, so I felt at home and comfortable), there arrived some notables of Reggio fresh from Rome, one of whom said he had been staying with Brutus and had left him at Naples. They brought a proclamation of Brutus and Cassius, and news that there was to be a full meeting of the Senate on the 1st, and that Brutus and Cassius had written to the ex-consuls and ex-praetors asking them to attend. They said there was good hope that Antony would yield, a settlement be reached, and our friends allowed to return to Rome. They added that I was missed, and somewhat censured. On hearing this, without a moment's hesitation, I abandoned the idea of crossing, which, God knows, I never much liked even before. . . .

On the 17th when I got back to Elea, Brutus, who was anchored in the River Heles three miles to the north, heard of it and came at once on foot to meet me. Lord, how delighted he was at my return, or rather turning back! He poured out everything he had previously repressed, and made me think of your words, 'Our friend Brutus makes no comment.' But he was most distressed that I had not been in the House on August 1. He praised Piso[1] to the skies, and said he was very glad I had removed the grounds for two serious criticisms. One of these I knew I was incurring by going abroad, that of despairing of the Republic and abandoning it (plenty of people had reproached me with tears in their eyes, and I could not convince them I should soon be back); the other reproach which Brutus and his companions (quite a number) were so glad I had avoided was that of going over, as people thought, to see the Olympic Games. That would indeed have been extremely reprehensible whatever the political situation, and unpardonable in the present crisis. You can imagine how grateful I was to that south wind for saving me from such a stigma! . . .

(*Ad Att.*, XVI, 7, 1; 5)

*To Tiro, from young Marcus Cicero*                          *Athens, August,* 44 B.C.

After looking forward terribly from day to day for the post to arrive, at last I have received my mail from home, forty-six days after you sent it off. I was simply delighted to get it. My dear, kind father's letter gave me the greatest pleasure, but your most charming enclosure put the crowning touch to my happiness. So I am no longer sorry for

1. Father of Julius Caesar's wife Calpurnia. He was now the first man to stand up against Antony.

the break in our correspondence, but actually glad, seeing that through omitting to write I have reaped such a harvest of kindness from you. I am also terribly glad that you accepted my excuse without hesitation.

I am sure, my dear old Tiro, that the rumours which reach you about me are all that you could desire. I will live up to them, and endeavour to see that this budding reputation of mine grows daily twice as good; so that you may with all faith and confidence fulfil your promise to be the trumpeter of my virtues; for the errors of my youth have brought me such pain and suffering that my mind shrinks from the memory of the things I did, and my ears detest the mention of them. In this worry and grief of mine I know from experience you have sympathised. And that does not surprise me, for you wished me all success not only for my own sake but also for yours, because it has always been my wish that you should share in any happiness of mine.

So since I have caused you pain, I shall now take care that the pleasure I cause you is twice as great. I must tell you that my relationship to Cratippus is very close, more like that of a son than a pupil; for not only do I like hearing his lectures, but I am terribly attracted by his own peculiar charm. I spend whole days with him, and often part of the night too, since I try to get him to dine with me as often as he possibly can. These relations having been established, he often surprises us when we are at dinner, and dropping the stern mask of philosophy joins in the fun like a very human being. So I must take steps to introduce you as soon as possible to so pleasant and admirable a man.

What shall I tell you about Bruttius? I never let him leave my side. He's so simple and austere in his way of life, and yet such delightful company (for our studies and our daily researches are not inconsistent with fun). I have taken lodgings for him next door and do my best from my meagre resources to subsidise his pittance.

Then I've begun declamation in Greek with Cassius; in Latin, however, I prefer to practise with Bruttius. The friends I go about with every day are pupils of Cratippus he brought from Mitylene; they are good scholars of whom he thinks very highly. I also see a good deal of Epicrates, head of the Athenians, and Leonides, and others of that sort. *Quant à moi, c'est tout.*

You mentioned Gorgias. I found him useful for ordinary declamation exercises, but I put obedience to my father's instructions above

G

all other considerations; and since my father had written expressly that I should dismiss Gorgias at once, I thought it best not to shilly-shally, in case any excessive enthusiasm on my part should arouse suspicions in his mind; besides, it also occurred to me that it would be a serious thing to set up my opinion against my father's. But I'm grateful for your welcome interest and advice.

I accept the excuse you made that you have no spare time, knowing how busy you always are. I am terribly glad you've bought the farm, and hope it will turn out to have been a good deal. Don't be surprised at my congratulating you on this so late in my letter. It was just as late in yours that you told me you had bought it. So you're a man of property! You'll have to drop those town manners: you've become a Roman country gentleman now! How clearly I can see your dear old face before me as I write; I seem to see you buying things for the farm, talking to your bailiff, saving the pips at dessert and putting them in your pocket. But with regard to the transaction itself, I am as sorry as you are that I could not help you out then. But you may be sure that I will come to your assistance if only fortune comes to mine, especially as I know the farm has really been bought for the benefit of us both.

Many thanks for taking trouble over my commissions. Please have a secretary sent out for me as quickly as possible, preferably a Greek; he could save me a great deal of labour by copying out my lecture-notes. But above all, take care of yourself, so that we may talk about books together again.

Please be nice to the bearer, Anteros.     (*Ad Fam.*, XVI, 21)

*Though Cicero arrived at Rome on August 31, he abstained from attending the Senate on September 1, when the deification of Caesar was on the agenda. Antony, who had recently married Clodius' widow, Fulvia, made a furious outburst against him for this. Cicero's response was the speech later known as the* First Philippic,[1] *a temperate but unmistakable declaration of war on Caesarianism. Antony replied on September 19 with a violent invective, which in turn provoked the* Second Philippic, *perhaps Cicero's most devastating speech, which was never delivered but was probably published as a pamphlet before the end of the year. His other*

1. Named after the famous speeches of Demosthenes against Philip of Macedon in the fourth century B.C.

*literary activities were unabated, and the two volumes* On Glory *(not extant) were followed by three volumes* On Duty *(De Officiis), which were written for his son.*

*At this point one letter deserves a place as representing the better element on the Caesarian-Antonian side. Gaius Matius was one of Cicero's oldest friends, but also a devoted friend of Caesar (see p. 160). After Caesar's death he supported Antony and Octavian as his successors. Cicero criticised him for this, and on hearing that he was aggrieved, wrote explaining his position. This is Matius' reply.*

*To Cicero, from Gaius Matius*              *Rome, end of August,* 44 B.C.

I was extremely glad to get your letter and learn that your opinion of me was what I had so earnestly hoped. Not that I had any real doubts, but I attached the greatest importance to it: hence my anxiety to keep it untarnished. I was sure I had not done anything that could offend any right-minded person, and this made me the less inclined to believe that anyone so endowed as yourself with every kind of admirable quality could have been lightly persuaded to listen to anything, especially in view of my cordial and long-standing attachment to you, which still continues.

Now that I am easy on that score, I will answer the allegations which you have so often rebutted on my behalf, as was to be expected in view of your exceptional goodness and of our friendship. I am well aware of what people have said against me since Caesar's death. They reproach me with my sorrow at the passing of an old friend and indignation at the death of one I loved. They assert that patriotism should be put above friendship, as though they had already proved that Caesar's removal had benefitted the State. But I will not try to be clever: I confess that I have not attained to their heights in philosophy. I did not follow Caesar in the civil conflict, but neither did I desert my friend because I disapproved of what he did. I never approved of the civil war, nor even of the cause of the dispute, but endeavoured to stifle it at birth. And so, when my friend proved victorious, I was not allured by promotion or money, whereas the others, with less claim on him than I, abused these rewards scandalously. Actually my own resources were diminished by that very law thanks to which many of those who now rejoice at Caesar's death were able to retain their position in the State. And I worked just as hard to save my compatriots on the defeated side as for my own salvation.

So how can I, who wanted everyone to be safe, fail to be indignant at the death of the man who conceded that desire, especially as the same men were responsible for his unpopularity and for his death? 'You will suffer then', they say, 'for daring to condemn what we have done.' What unheard-of insolence! Fancy some men boasting of a crime while others cannot even complain of it with impunity! Why even slaves have always been free to fear, rejoice or sorrow as they choose and not as someone else chooses; and now these 'champions of liberty' insist on trying to frighten us out of this. But they won't succeed. No fears for my personal safety will ever make me untrue to my duty and to the claims of humanity. I have never thought an honourable death was a thing to be avoided: often I have thought it a thing to be welcomed.

But why should they be annoyed if my only desire is that they should regret what they have done? I want everyone to feel sorrow for Caesar's death. They say that I ought, as a patriot, to wish the constitution preserved. So I do; but if my actions in the past and my hopes for the future do not prove it without words of mine, I cannot claim to demonstrate it by argument.

So in all earnestness I beg you to let facts speak louder than words, and, if you agree with me that honesty is the best policy, not to believe that I can ever have dealings with disloyal people. Or do you think that now, in my declining years, I should change the character I formed as a young man, when error would have been excusable, and undo my whole past? That I will not do. Nor yet will I go out of my way to give offence, apart from deploring the sad end of a dear friend of mine and a most distinguished man.

But even if my intentions were otherwise, I should never deny what I was doing, for fear of being considered both a criminal for my misdeeds and a cowardly hypocrite for my pretences. Then what about my arranging for the festival which the young Caesar gave in honour of his adoptive father's victory? That was a matter of private obligation, and had nothing to do with forms of government. In any case, I was bound to pay this tribute to the memory and eminence of a close friend, even after his death; nor could I refuse the request of a young man so full of promise and so worthy of the name of Caesar.

I have also frequently called on the consul Antony to pay my respects. You will find that those who accuse me of lack of patriotism are always going there, to ask for something or to pick up something. What impertinence! Caesar never put any obstacle in the way of my associating with whom I pleased, even with people he himself disliked; and now those who have robbed me of my friend endeavour by complaining of me to prevent my choosing my own associates.

But I am confident both that the circumspectness of my life will eventually prevail over false slanders, and that even those who dislike me for my loyalty to Caesar would rather have their friends be like me than like themselves. As for me, if my dreams come true I shall spend the remainder of my life in retirement at Rhodes; but if something crops up to prevent this, I shall still retain at Rome my preference for the right thing being done.

I am most grateful to Trebatius for being instrumental in bringing to light your frank and friendly feelings towards me, and for giving me still more cause to respect and esteem one whom I have always found it easy to like.

All my good wishes, and I trust I shall have yours.

                                                                          (*Ad Fam.*, XI, 28)

*To Cassius, near Naples*                    *Rome, late in September*, 44 B.C.
I am extremely delighted at your approval of my declaration and speech; if only I had more such chances there would be no trouble about restoring freedom and the constitution. But this damned madman, far more villainous than the man you claimed to be the greatest villain ever killed, is seeking an excuse for a massacre, and is alleging that I was originally responsible for Caesar's being put to death, simply in order to incite the ex-servicemen against me. Not that I fear this danger overmuch, so long as my reputation is enhanced by my sharing in the glory of your deed.

The result is that neither Piso, who unsupported made the first attack on Antony, nor I, who did the same a month later, nor Publius Servilius, who followed me closely, can enter the House with safety; for the swashbuckler is out for blood, and he imagined he would make a beginning with mine on September 19, on which day he turned up ready primed with a speech he had been studying for several days in the house that used to be Metellus'. But how could he study anything

in a den of vice and drunkenness? The result was that he struck everyone, in a phrase I have used to you before about him, as not delivering
his speech but disgorging it in his usual way.

So the answer to your assertion that you believe my eloquence
and prestige can do good is that, as far as our plight allows, some good
has indeed been done; the Roman people is at least aware now that
there are three ex-consuls who, because they have been loyal to the
Republic and spoken their minds, cannot enter the Senate with
safety. . . .                                                        (*Ad Fam.*, XII, 2, 1–2)

*To Atticus, at Rome*          *Pozzuoli, near Naples, November 2, 44* B.C.
When I know what day I shall be arriving, I will let you know. I've
got to wait for my heavy luggage, which is coming from Anagni,
and there's illness in my household.

On the evening of the 1st I got a letter from Octavian. He has
great schemes. He has won over the ex-servicemen at Casilinum and
Caserta to his way of thinking, which is not surprising, as he offers
them five hundred denarii apiece. He is thinking of touring the other
resettlement towns. Obviously his idea is war with Antony under
his leadership. So that I can see that in a few days time' we shall be
in arms.

But whom are we to follow? Look at his name![1] Look at his age!
Again, he begins by asking me to meet him secretly at Capua, of all
places. Childish, if he thinks that can be done secretly. I have written
to tell him that it is both unnecessary and impracticable. He sent me
one Caecina, a friend of his from Volterra, with news that Antony
with the Fifth Legion (the Larks) was setting out for Rome, levying
money from provincial boroughs, and marching with colours flying
at the head of his troops. He asked my advice whether he should start
for Rome with 3000 ex-servicemen, or hold Capua and intercept
Antony's advance, or join the three legions from Macedonia now
marching along the Adriatic coast. (He hopes these are for him: they
refused to accept a gratuity from Antony, or so he says, greeted him
with volleys of abuse, and left him when he tried to address them.)

In short, Octavian offers himself as our leader, and thinks we ought
to stand by him. My advice was that he should start for Rome, since

1. After he was adopted by Caesar in his will Octavius' name became Gaius
Julius Caesar Octavianus. He was now nineteen.

I think he is likely to have the city mob on his side, and the loyalists too, if he can gain their confidence. O Brutus, where are you now? What a golden opportunity you are missing! I didn't foresee just this, but I thought some such thing would happen.

Now I want your advice: shall I go to Rome or stay here, or take refuge at Arpino (that's the place for security)? To Rome, I think, for fear people may notice my absence when they see something big is happening. Do solve this riddle: I never was in such a dilemma.

*(Ad Att.,* XVI, 8)

*To Atticus, at Rome          Pozzuoli, near Naples, November* 5, 44 B.C.
  ... I did not bury myself in my house at Pompeii, as I told you I should, firstly because of the weather, which has been abominable, and secondly because I got a letter every day from Octavian urging me to take a hand in affairs, to come to Capua, to save the Republic a second time, and in any case to go at once to Rome. My state is of one

willing to wound and yet afraid to strike.

However, he certainly has been, and is, very active. He will come to Rome with a large following. But he's clearly a child. He thinks he can summon the Senate at once. But who will come? And if anyone does come, who will risk offending Antony until things become clearer? Perhaps he will prove a safeguard[1] on January 1, unless the conflict is over by then. It's wonderful how the provincial boroughs support the boy. On his way to Samnium he came to Calvi and stopped at Teano. The cheering crowds that greeted him were amazing. Would you believe it? That is why I shall go to Rome more quickly than I had intended. As soon as my plans are made, I will write. ...

*(Ad Att.,* XVI, 11, 6)

*Already in June Antony had put through a decree appointing himself governor of Hither Gaul instead of Decimus Brutus. On the news that two of the four legions he had recalled from Macedonia had gone over to Octavian he left Rome on November 28, marched north to his new province, and besieged Decimus in Modena.*

1. To the Senate. The new consuls, Hirtius and Pansa, would take office on January 1.

*Cicero now emerged once more as the leader of Rome. He rallied the
new consuls, the Senate and people with his* Philippics, *basing his policy
on the military support of Octavian, for whom he and others proposed
unusual honours. War was declared on Antony on February 2, 43.*

To Trebonius,[1]                                     *Rome, February 2, 43 B.C.*
*Governor of West Asia Minor*

How I wish you had invited me to that splendid banquet on the
Ides of March: there would then have been no leavings! As it is they
are causing us such trouble that we feel your immortal service to your
country left something to be desired. The fact that you, good man as
you are, took Antony aside that day, and that your kindness was
instrumental in keeping this pest alive, makes me sometimes feel
almost angry with you (though I have hardly the right); for the
trouble you left behind has fallen more heavily on me than on all the
rest put together.

As soon as the Senate could meet under free conditions after
Antony's most undignified departure, I resumed my spirit of former
days, which you and that wholehearted patriot, your father, have
always praised and prized. After the tribunes had moved that the
Senate should meet on December 20, on a further motion put by them
I reviewed the whole situation, and spoke with great vehemence; and
more by dint of passion than persuasion I recalled an assembly grown
torpid and effete to its former character and traditions. The events of
that day and my exertions and appeals were the first things that gave
the Roman people hope of recovering their freedom. And from then
on I have devoted every moment, not only to planning, but also to
acting, in the interests of the Republic.

If I did not assume that affairs in the capital and everything that
goes on is being reported to you, overwhelmed though I am with
work, I should write to you in full. But others will be telling you all
this, so I will only summarise a few facts. We have a determined
Senate, but of the ex-consuls some are timid and others disaffected.
We have suffered a great loss in the death of Servius Sulpicius. Lucius
Caesar's heart is in the right place, but being Antony's uncle he does
not propose extreme measures. The consuls, Hirtius and Pansa, are

1. Trebonius never got this letter: Dolabella, whom Antony sent off to oust
Cassius from the governorship of Syria, had him murdered at Smyrna.

excellent. Decimus Brutus is splendid. The boy Caesar[1] is excellent, and I have hopes he will continue to be. At any rate I can assure you that, if he had not quickly enrolled those ex-servicemen and if his influence had not detached two legions from Antony, and if Antony had not had the consequent danger to face, there is no crime of brutality he would have spared us.

Though I expect you have heard all this, I wanted you to have it confirmed. I will write more fully if I find I have time.

(Ad Fam., x, 28)

*During the next few months Cicero at Rome was the unifying force of the Republicans, urging them on and receiving their despatches. He corresponded with Brutus in the Balkan Peninsula, with Cassius in Syria, with Trebonius in Asia Minor, with Cornificius in North Africa, with Pollio in Spain, with Plancus and Lepidus in Further Gaul, with Galba and Decimus Brutus in Hither Gaul.*

*To Brutus, at Durazzo*                     Rome, *April* 17, 43 B.C.
    . . . You say I have been in no great haste to attack the Antonies and praise me for it. I believe you are sincere in this, but I cannot by any means accept the distinction you draw when you say that more energy should be applied to preventing civil war than in venting anger on the losers. I disagree with you violently, Brutus; I do not admit your doctrine of mercy; a salutary severity outweighs all its superficial and hollow advantages; if we are going to be merciful, civil wars will never cease. But that will be your affair: I can say with the father in Plautus' *Trinummus*:

> My time of life is almost done; the future, it is yours.

You'll be crushed, believe me, Brutus, if you don't take care. You won't always find the people thus, nor the Senate, nor find such a leader of the Senate. Think of these as the words of the Delphic Oracle. None could be more true.        (*Brut.* VIII, 2/1, 2, 5–6)

*Two great battles for Modena were now fought. On April* 14 *or* 15

---

    1. Note that Cicero now consents to call him so, whereas Brutus continues to call him Octavius (not even Octavian).

*Mark Antony defeated Pansa but was worsted by Hirtius. Caesar Octavian successfully defended the camp against Lucius Antony. On April 21 Decimus Brutus sallied out and defeated Antony decisively, though Hirtius was killed and Pansa shortly afterwards died of wounds. Antony escaped, however, and outwitted his opponents.*

*The following letter was written after the news of the first battle.*

*To Brutus, at Durazzo*                                    *Rome, April 21, 43 B.C.*

Our position seems better now. I presume you have had reports of what has happened. The consuls have shown themselves the sort of men I have often told you they are. The boy Caesar has natural strength of character to an extraordinary degree; I only hope that when he is at the height of honour and popularity we may be able to guide and control him as easily as we have controlled him up to now! This will certainly be harder, but I have good hopes; for the lad has been convinced, principally by me, that we owe our safety to him—and it is true that, if he had not turned Antony away from the capital, all would have been lost.

Three or four days before this splendid victory the whole city population, seized by a kind of panic, was for streaming out with their wives and children to join you: the same people, on April 20, were more in favour of your coming here than of their going to you. On that day I reaped my crowning reward for all my labours and my sleepless nights—if there can be any reward in well-founded and genuine glory: the whole population of the city came flocking round me, carried me right up to the Capitol with tremendous shouting and cheering and then set me on the platform in the Forum. I have no vanity in me—nor should I have—yet a demonstration in which all classes join and a gesture of gratitude and congratulation does move me, because it is a glorious thing for me to be the people's hero in their hour of deliverance. But I should prefer you to hear of this from others. . . .                                            (*Brut.* IX, 1–2/1, 3, 1–2)

*Antony, 'beaten from Modena', made good his escape across the Alps, showing great courage and resource. (Cf. Caesar Octavian's reminder, Shakespeare, A. and C. I, iv, 56–71.) Lepidus, Brutus' brother-in-law, went over to Antony soon afterwards, and was declared a public enemy on June 30.*

*To Cicero, at Rome, from Pollio*[1]          *Cordova, Spain, June 8, 43 B.C.*

My quaestor, the younger Balbus, having drawn a large sum of ready money, and collected a great quantity of bullion and a still greater of silver from the public revenues, decamped from Cadiz without even paying the troops. After being held up off Gibraltar for three days by the weather he crossed over on June 1 to the kingdom of Bogud of Tangiers, with his pockets lined nicely. Amid conflicting rumours— and every time a message comes the brute has changed his plans—I don't know yet whether he is returning to Cadiz or going to Rome.

But besides his embezzlement and looting and flogging of allied persons, listen to what he has done—just like Caesar, as he always boasts: on the last day of a festival he got up at Cadiz he presented an actor called Herennius Gallus with a knight's gold ring and conducted him to a seat in the first fourteen rows which he had reserved for the knights. He extended his own tenure of the office of Borough Commissioner.[2] He held elections for two years on successive days, i.e. he returned whoever he chose. He restored exiles, men banished not in recent times but in the mutiny under Sextus Varus when the local senate was massacred or expelled.

For what follows, however, even Caesar provided no precedent. In the course of the festival he put on a historical play about the mission he himself undertook in order to try to win over the pro-consul Lentulus to Caesar[3]; and during the performance he was so stirred by the memory of his exploits that he burst into tears. At a gladiatorial show a soldier of Pompey's called Fadius, who had been pressed into the troop and had twice beaten his man without being paid, refused to sign on and took refuge in the crowd. Balbus first of all ordered Gallic cavalry to charge the crowd, since stones had been thrown at him while Fadius was being dragged away, and then, having carried the man off, buried him up to the waist in the gladiators' school and burnt him alive. He himself meanwhile, having lunched, strolled about in his slippers with his tunic undone and his hands behind his back, and when the poor wretch shrieked 'I am a Roman

1. Governor of Spain. This notable literary figure was praised as a boy by Catullus and as a man by his friends and protégés Virgil and Horace.

2. Balbus was a Spaniard and a native of Cadiz.

3. See p. 116.

Citizen', answered, 'Go off, then, and appeal to the people.' He has also thrown Roman citizens to the wild beasts, among them a pedlar who frequented sales, a man well-known in Seville because he was deformed. This is the kind of monster I've had to deal with. But I'll tell you more when we meet.

Now for the main point. You people must decide what you want me to do. I have three reliable legions. One of them, the Twenty-eighth, had been incited by Antony to join him at the beginning of the war with promises that on the day it entered his camp he would give each man five hundred denarii, and that in the day of victory he would give them the same gratuities as his own legions (and who is not aware that these would know no bounds?). The troops were very much worked up, but I retained them (God knows, it was hard). I could not have done it if they had been concentrated, for certain isolated units actually did mutiny. The other legions too he was continually working on by means of letters and unlimited promises. And Lepidus also was pressing me quite as hard, writing and getting Antony to write, to let him have the Thirtieth Legion.

This army then, which I was unwilling to sell at any price, nor to deplete under threat of what would happen to me if these two won, you may reckon as retained and kept safe for the Republic; and since I have carried out what were your orders, I beg you to believe that I should have carried out anything else you had ordered. I have kept Spain at peace and the army subject to my discipline; I have never crossed the borders of my province; I have despatched no regular, or even auxiliary, soldier anywhere else, and have punished any cavalry I found trying to desert.

For all this I shall think I have sufficient reward if the Republic is preserved. All the same, if the Republic and the majority of the Senate had known me better, they would have been able to use me to greater advantage.

P.S. I am sending for your perusal a letter I wrote to Balbus while he was still in the province. I have also written a historical play for which, if you would care to read it, you may ask my friend Cornelius Gallus.[1]                                      (*Ad Fam.*, x, 32)

---

1. Virgil's friend, the great elegiac poet, whose works were suppressed after his disgrace and suicide in 26 B.C.

*To Atticus, at Rome,*               *Macedonia, middle of June,* 43 B.C.
*from Brutus*

You say in your letter that Cicero is surprised at my never making any comment on his actions. Since you ask me, I feel obliged to tell you what I think.

I know Cicero has done everything with the best intentions: from experience I could hardly fail to appreciate his devotion to the Republic as much as anything. But he sometimes acts—can one say 'tactlessly' of a man so eminently prudent, or 'selfishly' of a man who for the sake of the Republic did not hesitate to incur the enmity of Antony in all his power? I don't know what to say to you but this: the boy's ambition and highhandedness have been stimulated rather than curbed by Cicero; and he carries this partiality to such a pitch that he does not refrain from abusive remarks, which often, indeed, recoil on him with double force; thus he put more than one person to death himself, so he ought to admit himself to be a murderer before calling Casca the names he does. He is treating Casca as Bestia once treated himself. Just because we are not bragging in season and out of the Ides of March in the way he is always talking about his Nones of December,[1] is Cicero in any better position to malign a most glorious deed than Bestia and Clodius were to be for ever criticising the things he did as consul?

Our friend Cicero boasts to me that he, a civilian, withstood the military power of Antony. What good is that to me if the price demanded for crushing Antony is Antony's place for a successor, and if the chastiser of that evil comes forward as the supporter of another likely, unless we prevent it, to have still firmer foundations and deeper roots? Even supposing his policy is dictated by fear of tyranny, or a tyrant, I cannot feel grateful to a man who, in order to avoid being slave to a particular ill-tempered master, refrains from deprecating slavery itself; and worse than that, proposes to give a new master a Triumph and pay for his troops, and by decrees of every kind encourages him not to be ashamed to covet the position once held by the man whose name he has adopted. Is this worthy of an ex-consul, or of Cicero? . . .

So, although Octavius may call Cicero 'father', consult him in everything, praise him and thank him, yet it will become clear that his acts do not tally with his words. For what can be more repugnant to

1. December 5, 63, when Cicero executed the Catilinarians.

common sense than to treat a man as a father who is not even to be
reckoned among the free? And yet this worthy man, to gain Octavius'
favour, is going in that direction, doing all he can, hastening to that
end. For my part I set no store by those accomplishments at which I
know Cicero is a past master: what good has he been done by all those
fulsome writings of his about freedom for the fatherland, and about
honour, death, exile and poverty? How much better versed in these
things is Philippus, who refused to concede to his stepson what Cicero
concedes to him though he is no relation! So let him cease aggravating
our troubles by his boasting: for what does it help us that Antony has
been beaten, if the only result is that another steps into his shoes?
And, even as it is, there is a note of uncertainty in your letter.

Long live Cicero indeed (and well he may!), to cringe and serve, if
he is not ashamed to think of his age and rank and past achievements!
I at any rate will be deterred by no conditions of slavery, however
favourable, from fighting against the principle, that is, against tyranny
and unconstitutional powers and despotism and authority that sets
itself up above the laws. Even though Octavius[1] may be a good man,
as you say, though I have never thought so, yet our ancestors willed
that no one, not even a father, should have absolute mastery.

If I were not as devoted to you as Cicero thinks Octavius is to him,
I should not have written this to you. It hurts me to think of you
getting angry as you read it, you who are so fond of all your friends,
and especially of Cicero. But believe me when I say that my personal
feelings for Cicero are in no way diminished, though my opinion of
him is very much so, since you cannot expect a man to form an
opinion save according to his lights.

I wish you had told me what proposals of marriage my dear Attica
has had.[2] I could have given you some idea of what I thought. I am
not surprised you are anxious about my Portia's health. Finally, I will
gladly do what you asked, for my sisters ask the same, and I know the
man and what he wants.                          (*Brut.* xxv/I, 17, 1–2; 5–7)

*To Brutus, in Macedonia*                    *Rome, middle of July,* 43 B.C.
. . . I think it would be not out of place if I explained here what aim

1. If that is the right reading.
2. She was eight or nine years old, and later married Agrippa. Roman girls
were often betrothed early.

I have pursued in my proposals in the Senate during this war. You will not have forgotten, Brutus, my representations since Caesar's death and your memorable Ides of March about your omission and about the storm threatening the Republic; you had banished a great plague, wiped out a great stain on the Roman people, and won immortal glory for your own names, but the machine of domination was handed on to Lepidus and Antony, the former pre-eminent for treachery, the latter for corruption, both of them afraid of peace and hostile to tranquillity. Against these men, who were inflamed with a passion for revolution, we had no bulwark to set up.

The State had with one accord risen to maintain its freedom. I was at the time too violent, whereas you, perhaps more prudently, left the city you had liberated and declined the proffered support of Italy. Accordingly, seeing that the capital was in the hands of cut-throats, and that neither you nor Cassius could live there with safety, and that Antony was holding it down by force, I thought it was time for me to get away from it myself (it was a grim sight to see the city held down by criminals with all power of rescue cut off); but my heart was as firmly rooted as ever in love of my country, and I could not bear to leave it in its hour of danger. So when, in the midst of my voyage to Greece, a seasonable south wind, as though protesting against my purpose, had brought me back to Italy, and I met you at Elea, the meeting greatly distressed me; for you were leaving, Brutus—I say 'leaving', since our Stoics won't allow that the wise man ever runs away.

When I got to Rome, I at once stood up against Antony's criminal madness; and when this roused him against me, I began to conceive a truly Brutus-like plan (for this is the speciality of your family) of liberating the Republic.

The rest of the story is too long to tell, and must be passed over because I am the subject. I will only say this much: this lad Caesar, to whom, if we are honest, we must admit that we owe our continued existence, has had the springs of his action in my policy. To him I caused honours to be voted, but none that were not merited, Brutus, and none that were not inevitable. For as soon as we began to recover our liberty, before even the supreme excellence of Decimus Brutus had stirred itself and so brought home the fact to us, while our only protection was in the boy who had saved our necks from Antony, what honour was too great to decree him? Nevertheless all I then proposed was a vote of thanks, and that in quite moderate terms; I also proposed he should be given the status of military commander, which did seem a great honour for one of his age, but a necessary one for the control of an army (for what use is an army without the authority to command?). Philippus proposed a statue, Servius seniority for purposes of qualifying for office, and later Servilius still more seniority. Nothing seemed then too good for him.

But somehow men are more apt to behave generously in time of danger than gratefully after victory. Thus when that day of joy for the Republic dawned on which Decimus Brutus was relieved at Modena, and by a coincidence it was also his birthday, I proposed that the name of Brutus should be inserted in the official calendar under that date. I was only following a precedent set by our ancestors, who granted this honour to the woman Larentia[1] at whose altar in the Velabrum you priests regularly sacrifice; and in proposing a similar honour to Decimus my intention was that a most welcome victory should be commemorated for ever in the calendar. But on that day I discovered that there were rather more jealous men than grateful in the Senate.

In the course of those same days I lavished, if you will, honours upon the dead, Hirtius and Pansa, and even Aquila; and who could complain except the man who forgets past dangers when the fear is past? And I had another motive besides grateful recognition of past services: for the benefit of posterity I wanted there to exist an eternal record of the public execration of these ruthless enemies.

My next act will not, I suspect, commend itself so much to you, seeing that it was not approved by friends of yours who are excellent characters but inexperienced in statecraft: I proposed an Ovation[2] for young Caesar. But for my part—though I may be wrong, and I am not the sort of man to cling to opinions simply because they are mine— I think this was as good a proposal as any I have made during the war. Why it should be so, I must not disclose, in case I should seem to have acted more out of foresight than gratitude. . . .

(*Brut.* XXIII/I, 15, 4–9)

1. A legendary figure, wife of the shepherd who brought up Romulus and Remus.

2. A secondary form of Triumph.

# Epilogue

*Alas for Cicero's foresight! Caesar Octavian, slighted by the Senate, marched to Rome, demanded one of the consulships left vacant by the death of Hirtius and Pansa, and obtained it on August 19, his kinsman Pedius receiving the other. He proceeded to revoke the outlawry of Antony and Dolabella and to secure the condemnation of Julius Caesar's assassins. Brutus was still in Macedonia, having rejected repeated appeals from Cicero and Decimus that he should bring his army to Italy.*

*Caesar Octavian now openly joined Antony, and in November, on a river-island near Bologna, formed the Second Triumvirate with him and Lepidus. The three proceeded to outlaw their political opponents. Mark Antony, unable to forgive the* Second Philippic, *demanded Cicero, and Octavian failed to protect him. Three hundred Senators and two thousand knights lost their lives in this 'Proscription'.*

*The rest of the story will best be told by Plutarch, in the translation of Sir Thomas North, which Shakespeare used.*

'While these matters were a-brewing, Cicero was at a house of his in the country, by the city of Tusculum, having at home with him also his brother, Quintus Cicero. News being brought them thither of these proscriptions or outlawries, appointing men to be slain, they determined to go to Astura, a place by the seaside where Cicero had another house, there to take sea, and from thence to go into Macedon unto Brutus. For there ran a rumour that Brutus was very strong, and had a great power. So they caused themselves to be conveyed thither in two litters, both of them being so weak with sorrow and grief that they could not otherwise have gone their ways. As they were on their way, both their litters going as near to each other as they could, they bewailed their miserable state; but Quintus chiefly, who took it most grievously. For remembering that he took no money with him when he came from his house, and that Cicero his brother also had very little for himself, he thought it best that Cicero should hold on his journey, whilst he himself made an errand home to fetch such things as he lacked, and so to make haste again to overtake his brother. They both thought it best so, and then tenderly embracing one another, the tears falling from their eyes, they took leave of each other. Within a few days after Quintus Cicero, being betrayed by his own servants unto them that made search for him, he was cruelly slain, and his son with him.

'But Marcus Tullius Cicero, being carried unto Astura, and there finding a ship ready, embarked immediately and sailed along the coast unto Mount Circeii, having a good gale of wind. There, the mariners determining forthwith to make sail again, he came ashore, either for fear of the sea or for that he had some hope that Caesar had not altogether forsaken him; and therewithal returning towards Rome by land, he had gone about a hundred furlongs thence. But then, being at a strait how to resolve and suddenly changing his mind, he would needs be carried back again to the sea, where he continued all night marvellous sorrowful and full of thoughts. For one while he was in mind to go secretly unto Octavius Caesar's house, and to kill himself by the hearth of his chimney, to make the Furies of Hell to revenge his blood; but being afraid to be intercepted by the way and cruelly handled, he turned from that determination.

'Then falling into other unadvised determinations, being perplexed as he was, he put himself again into his servants' hands, to be conveyed by sea to another place called Gaeta. There he had a very proper pleasant summer-house, where the north winds called Etesian do give a trim fresh air in the summer season. In that place also there is a little temple dedicated to Apollo, not far from the seaside. From thence there came a great shoal of crows making a marvellous noise, that came flying towards Cicero's ship, which rowed upon the shore side. This shoal of crows came and lighted upon the yard of their sail, some crying, and some pecking at the cords with their bills, so that every man judged straight that this was a sign of ill-luck at hand.

Cicero, notwithstanding this, came ashore, and went into his house, and laid down to see if he could sleep. But the most part of these crows came and lighted upon the chamber window where he lay, making a wonderful great noise; and some of them got into Cicero's bed where he lay, the clothes being cast over his head, and they never left him, till little by little they had with their bills plucked off the clothes that covered his face. His men, seeing that, and saying to themselves that they were too vile beasts if they would tarry to see their master slain before their eyes, considering that brute beasts had care to save his life, seeing him so unworthily entreated, and that they should not do the best they could to save his life, partly by entreaty and partly by force they put him again into his litter to carry him to the sea.

'But in the meantime came the murderers appointed to kill him, Herennius a centurion and Popilius Laenas, tribune of the soldiers (whose cause Cicero had once pleaded before the judges, when he was accused for the murder of his own father), having soldiers attending upon them. So, Cicero's gate being shut, they entered the house by force, and missing him, they asked them of the house what had become of him. They answered, they could not tell. Howbeit there was a young boy in the house called Philologus, a slave enfranchised by Quintus Cicero, whom Tullius Cicero had brought up in the Latin tongue, and had taught him the liberal sciences. He told this Herennius that his servants carried him in a litter towards the sea, through dark narrow lanes shadowed with wood on either side. Popilius the colonel, taking some soldiers with him, ran about on the outside of the lanes to take him at his coming out of them, and Herennius on the other side entered the lanes. Cicero, hearing him coming, commanded his men to set down his litter; and taking his beard in his left hand, as his manner was, he stoutly looked the murderers in the faces, his head and beard being all white, and his face lean and wrinkled, for the extreme sorrows he had taken. Divers of them that were by held their hands before their eyes while Herennius did cruelly murther him. So, Cicero, being three-score and four years of age, thrust his neck out of the litter, and had his head cut off by Antonius' commandment, and his hands also which wrote the orations called the Philippics against him.

'When these poor dismembered members were brought to Rome, Antonius by chance was busily occupied at that time about the election of certain officers; who, when he heard of them and saw them, he cried out aloud that now all his outlawries and proscriptions were executed; and thereupon commanded his head and hands should straight be set up over the pulpit for orations, in the place called Rostra. This was a fearful and horrible sight to the Romans, who thought they saw, not Cicero's face, but an image of Antonius' life and disposition. . . .

'Howbeit I understand that Caesar Augustus long time after that went one day to see one of his nephews, who had a book in his hand of Cicero's; and he, fearing lest his uncle would be angry to find that book in his hands, thought to hide it under his gown. Caesar saw it and took it from him, and read the most part of it standing, and then delivered it to the young boy and said to him: "He was a wise man indeed, my child, and loved his country well".'

# GLOSSARY OF TECHNICAL TERMS

ACADEMY. See NEW ACADEMY.

AEDILE. Second rung of four on the ladder of high office. The four aediles were supintendents of public places and the activities that took place in them. Election was for the ensuing year only.

CAESAR'S LAW. The *Lex Iulia De Repetundis* forbade governors on travel to exact anything for their own use except wood, salt and hay.

COMPITALIA. Winter festival of the Lares, celebrated at crossroads.

CONSUL. The two consuls were the joint heads of the Roman Republic. Election was for the ensuing year only.

DICTATOR. Magistrate appointed in an emergency with supreme power.

EPICUREAN. Follower of Epicurus' philosophy of pleasure based on rationalism, materialism and quietism.

FASCES. Axes in bundles of rods carried by the bodyguard (*lictors*) of holders of the right of command (*imperium*).

FREEDMAN. Slave set free by his master, often remaining in the household.

GABINIUS' LAW. Forbade Romans to lend money to provincials.

GREAT MOTHER. *Alias* Cybele or Rhea; orgiastic deity of Asia Minor who had a foothold in Rome also.

IDES. The 15th of March, May, July and October, 13th of every other month.

IMPERATOR. Title conferred by acclamation of soldiers in the field on their victorious general.

IMPERIUM. Power of command possessed by a dictator, consul, pro-consul or praetor. Governors of provinces retained it until entering the city boundary of Rome, after which they became ineligible for a Triumph. *Lictors* and *fasces* were the symbol of *imperium*.

KNIGHTS. The *Equites*, powerful class of rich business men who ranked next after the Senate.

LATIN FESTIVAL. The *Feriae Latinae*, held annually on the Alban Mount south of Rome.

LATIN RIGHTS. *Ius Latii*, the highest status short of Roman Citizenship to which allies could attain.

LEAP-MONTH. 'Intercalary' month periodically inserted to correct the calendar before Caesar reformed it radically.

LEGION. Military unit with a nominal establishment of about 6000.

LICTOR. Member of bodyguard of magistrate holding right of command (*imperium*), carrying *fasces* as insignia.

NEW ACADEMY. The eclectic philosophic school at Athens to which Cicero adhered.

NONES. The 7th of March, May, July and October, 5th of every other month.

PALINODE. Recantation.

PLEBEIAN. The *plebs*, originally inferior class, but by Cicero's day long since indistinguishable from *patricii* in respect of political rights. Tribunes had to be plebeians.

PRAETOR. Third rung of four on the ladder of high office. The eight praetors were the chief judicial magistrates. Election was for the ensuing year only.

PROSCRIPTION. Wholesale notice of outlawry; massacre of named individuals.

PROVINCES. The administrative departments of the Roman Empire outside Italy proper.

QUAESTOR. First rung of four on the ladder of high office. The twenty quaestors were paymasters. Election was for the ensuing year only.

ROSCIAN LAW. Reserved fourteen rows of seats in the theatre for the Knights.

ROSTRA. The platform in the Forum from which speeches were delivered.

SEMPRONIAN LAW. Required the Senate to specify, before consuls were elected, which province they were to govern between them after their year of office.

SENATE. The chief council of the Roman Republic, several hundred strong. Its resolutions carried great weight, and it had wide executive powers.

SESTERTIUM. A sum of money worth something between £10 and £30 at present values.

STOIC. Follower of philosophy inaugurated by Zeno about 300 B.C. which laid stress on virtue, duty and self-control.

SULLA'S LAW. The *Lex Cornelia De Provinciis Ordinandis* prescribed that there must not be more than thirty days' overlap of governors in a province.

THANKSGIVING SERVICE. *Supplicatio*, a public religious ceremony with processions, hymns and prayers.

TRIBUNE. The ten Tribunes of the Plebs were originally the people's watchdogs to check the Senate, each armed with a veto; later used as agents by the Senate or by factions in the game of politics.

TRIBUNE OF THE SOLDIERS. Officer roughly equivalent to colonel.

TRIUMPH. Successful general's procession with captives and booty through Rome, a much-coveted honour.

TRIUMVIR. One of ruling committee of three. Pompey, Caesar and Crassus formed the first, Antony, Octavian and Lepidus the second.

TWENTY COMMISSIONERS. Appointed by Caesar to carry out his Land Bill for resettling ex-servicemen.

VALUATION-LANDS. A law of Caesar's compelled creditors to accept debtors' land in payment, such land being valued at pre-war price (about 25 per cent lower).

# INDEX OF PROPER NAMES

*(To save space, a number of insignificant references have been omitted)*

## Q

## R

## S